LOOKING BACK AT BRITAIN

ROAD TO
RECOVERY

1950s

ROAD TO RECOVERY

1950s

Brian Moynahan

 Reader's Digest   gettyimages

CONTENTS

1950s IMAGE GALLERY

COVER, FRONT: Waiting for the launch of SS *Uganda* at Clydeside shipyard, March 1952.

COVER, BACK: A break for tea at a hound trail race at Troutbeck in the Lake District, September 1951.

TITLE PAGE: In Battle of Britain week, 1954, three children get a close-up view of an RAF Short Sunderland Mark V flying boat moored on the Thames near the Tower of London.

OPPOSITE: A resident of Morpeth Street in London's East End scrubs down her front steps in preparation for the coronation celebrations in June 1953.

FOLLOWING PAGES:

Three women in matching hats enjoy the fun fair at Battersea Park during the Festival of Britain, June 1951.

Football fans watching Arsenal in action against Glasgow Rangers at Highbury on 1 December, 1951.

Blowing balloons until they burst at Uncle Bertie's talent spotting contest in Eastbourne, August 1950.

Boys take a leap into the water, on holiday on the Norfolk Broads in May 1957.

FROM FESTIVAL TO TRAGEDY

A dazzling optimism was about to break through, but as the decade began, rationing and queues were as much a part of life as they had been during the war. The resentment of drabness showed in the first major event of 1950 – the February general election.

ATTLEE'S LAST YEARS IN OFFICE

Labour had won a landslide victory five years before. To public acclaim, they had gone a long way to slaying the 'Five Giants' identified by William (later, Lord) Beveridge in his famous reports on social services: Want, Disease, Ignorance, Squalor and Idleness.

Most of the welfare state as we still know it was put in place by Clement Attlee and his ministers in that post-war Labour government. The National Health Service (NHS) provided universal health care. State secondary education was free for all. The State was building social housing on council estates. The very young, the handicapped and problem families would be helped by social workers. There were new unemployment and sickness benefits, family allowances, free school dinners and milk. Yet the government that had done all this barely scraped back at the polls, its majority slashed from 146 to just five. The next year, it was gone.

Rationing ... and more rationing

The seemingly endless austerity was the main reason. Food rationing ended in West Germany on 6 January, 1950. In victorious Britain, though, everything except preserves was still on ration. An adult had an ounce and a half of cheese a week, an ounce of cooking fat, six ounces of butter, eight ounces of sugar, two pints of milk and one egg. To the dismay of children everywhere, sweets, which had gone off-ration in April 1949, were restricted again by August. 'Unexpected demand' was blamed, a poor excuse in a nation that had not been able to indulge its notoriously sweet tooth for almost a decade.

The meat ration was at its lowest ever level. During the war, it had stood at 87 per cent of pre-war consumption. The government now cut it to 69 per cent. The reason was a breakdown in talks with Argentina, which supplied much of the imported beef. The Conservatives seized the publicity opportunity and splashed the matchbox-sized meat ration across its election campaign posters. The bacon ration, too, was less than in the war, down to three ounces a week, or three medium-cut rashers, which was not going to make a government popular in a country that retained a folk memory of the full English breakfast.

In fact, the 1950 British diet was pretty healthy – and certainly healthier than that of 1939. It had sufficient, not excess, protein and energy value, and it was low in sugar and fat, including the highly saturated sort that would later be linked to cardiovascular disease. But nonetheless the impression was of a country on a permanent enforced diet, where the only little luxuries came from a barrow boy or the black market. Even margarine was rationed. Women in particular were fed up with ration coupons – not surprising, as they were the ones who did most of the queuing – and they turned against Labour in large numbers.

Of taxes and class and education

As to their husbands, the more they earned, the more they were aggrieved by high taxes. After the war Aneurin Bevan, Welsh firebrand and hard-core Socialist,

MAN OF THE PEOPLE

Prime Minister Clement Attlee – seen below at Edinburgh Road school, a polling station in Walthamstow – won a second term in February 1950, but with a much-reduced majority of just five seats. He remained a popular figure among the public, but before long his health would fail.

Then as now, polling stations were set up in village halls and schools around the country. This one (right) is at Stisted, Near Braintree in Essex. Long before the invention of the buggy, babies travelled in the snug comfort of a pram, looking back towards their mothers rather than facing out towards a busy, hostile world.

SCHOOL SCENES

THE BEST DAYS OF YOUR LIFE

Under the State system, children went to the local primary school until they were 11. Then they sat the 'eleven plus' exam. Those who did best got into grammar school. The eager young boys at Manchester GS (above) were taught by a master in a gown, a sign of his academic distinction. The equipment in the science labs at Beckenham and Penge GS is evidence of the same excellence. Some pupils went to vocational technical schools, but the majority went to secondary modern schools. Fully comprehensive schools, taking children of all abilities, were rare – at the start of the 1950s, there were only 20.

Critics of the grammar school system said that it was biased in favour of middle class children and that it was unfair to brand so many 11 year olds as 'failures'. Supporters said that education should not be dumbed down by having one standard for all if Britain was to retain high standards in the arts and sciences. Few boys – only one in 25 – went to university, and even fewer girls. The emphasis for them was on 'home skills', such as cooking and sewing, made to sound more educational as 'domestic science'.

had reputedly said to one Tory grandee: 'My class is on the up and yours is on the down.' Strictly speaking, that was not true in education, where class still certainly counted.

Nationally, in 1950 about a quarter of children were getting into grammar schools – though the figure was as high as 40 per cent in Westmoreland and as low as 10 per cent in Sunderland – and of these it was estimated that 60 per cent were the children of professionals and businessmen. Only 10 per cent were working class children, though they accounted for three-quarters of the school population. Class advantage was even more pronounced in tertiary education; even by the end of the decade, just over 4 per cent went on to university.

> 'My class is on the up and yours is on the down.'
>
> Aneurin Bevan

But in taxation, Bevan was undoubtedly right. He was the health minister who had created the NHS and it needed to be paid for. So did all the nationalised industries – coal, steel, railways, electricity, gas, water – and the continuing welfare reforms. Free legal aid was added in 1950.

There was never much doubt about who would pay the lion's share. By 1950, the real incomes of the wealthiest 100,000 people in the country were down almost two-thirds compared to pre-war levels. For the top million, the drop was more than a third. Surtax, a 'supertax' applied to the larger incomes, reached 97.5 per cent. A single man earning £10,000 a year in 1937 took home £6222 after paying tax and surtax. Under post-war Labour, this fell to £3501. On top of this, inflation had almost halved the value of the pound.

Bevan's grandees were pursued beyond the grave. Death duties were levied at 75 per cent on those assets they had preserved, which was 10 per cent more than in the war itself. One result was the break-up of landed estates, small and large, and the dereliction, often demolition, of stately homes. Many of these were no longer very stately, having been commandeered during the war for the billeting of troops. Some had housed guards for Italian and German prisoners of war, whose Nissen huts disfigured once elegant parkland.

From service to industry

Another consequence was the disappearance of the army of around 2 million domestic servants who had once worked in the grand homes and gardens. Even middle-income earners had often enjoyed the luxury of live-in help before the war, but with the standard rate of income tax at 47.5 per cent – and with competition for labour from the higher-paying factories and service industries – few could now afford it.

This had its knock-on effects, too, giving a fillip to the burgeoning market for labour-saving domestic machines. The market boomed for washing machines, vacuum cleaners and electric irons. The appearance of the lady of the house in the kitchen and garden also led to a boom in cookery and gardening books, and new radio programmes like *Gardeners' Question Time*.

It was not only traditional Tory voters whom taxes were hurting. Herbert Morrison, the deputy prime minister, warned of the consequences. 'The incentive to effort for workers as well as professional people and employers is seriously affected,' he said. The government was 'pressing on the limits of the taxpayers' endurance'. Or beyond it, so it soon transpired.

A NEW ROYAL BABY
In more care-free days before inheriting the throne, Princess Elizabeth shows off her new baby, Anne, born on 15 August, 1950. A very young Charles stands between his grandmother and his great-grandmother, Queen Mary, while the proud and happy father, Prince Philip, looks on.

A GREAT POWER OVER-STRETCHED

Britain was still a Great Power – at least in terms of the size of the bills that came in. Part of the financial strain came from running sterling as the world's second reserve currency, after the dollar. A third of the country's overseas investments had been sacrificed to pay for the war, but it still had to finance the defence of a worldwide empire. On top of that were the demands of the welfare state. No wonder there was a 'sterling crisis', a constant theme throughout the 1950s and well beyond.

The devaluation of the pound – it had recently fallen from $4.00 to $2.80 – meant less to individuals than it would today. Nobody was flying to Miami on holiday; few would even cross the Channel to visit the Continent they had so recently liberated. But devaluation had a huge impact on the press and on politics. Instinctively, the British felt the Sterling Area – that is, the number of countries that pegged their currency to the pound – to be part of their continuing greatness, and they were distressed at sterling's travails.

Commitments overseas

Military spending reflected Britain's huge and far-flung commitments and bore heavily on the taxpayer. Defence accounted for a thumping 10 per cent of national production, some of which went to pay for HMS *Ark Royal*, a new aircraft carrier launched in May 1950, replacing its namesake which had been torpedoed in 1941. It also hit the young men who were called up to military service. In September 1950, national service was extended. Instead of 18 months, conscripts now had to serve for two years – more if they went into the navy – and a further period was spent in the reserves.

The immediate trigger for the increase was the outbreak of war in Korea, after the communists in the North swept down across the 38th parallel into the South. Only the Americans made a larger contribution to the Western effort in the Cold War against the communist world. A largely British-manned Commonwealth division was fighting in Korea. British troops were in the Malayan jungle, tracking communist insurgents. In Europe, meanwhile, the men of the BAOR – dull as an acronym, but redolent in full as the British Army of the Rhine – were ex-enemies

continued on page 27

PUBLIC PROTEST

The British had refined protest down the years into well-conducted and generally well-behaved marches, often large, but sometimes very small and of baffling purpose to onlookers.

EQUAL PAY
The formidable masked campaigner Mrs Edith Goulden Bach shows haughty disdain for a police sergeant as he reaches for his notebook on the Strand in 1952. She was one of a group of similarly masked women demonstrating to promote a meeting of the campaign for equal pay and rights for women. Although by 1950 both the Conservative and Labour parties had endorsed equal pay in principle, neither had made any commitment to do anything about it. As a first step, in 1955 the Conservative government promised to introduce equal pay in stages in the public services, partly to prevent Labour using the issue to win women's votes. Action in the private sector was still years in the future.

EQUAL PAY CAMPAIGN COMMITTEE

JUSTICE FOR WOMEN

Equal Pay for Equal Work
The Rate for the job

THE RT. HON.   SPEAKERS:

Dr. EDITH SUMMERSKILL, M.P.
Miss IRENE WARD, C.B.E., M.P.
Mrs. CLEMENT DAVIES
Mrs. THELMA CAZALET-KEIR, C.B.E.
(CHAIRMAN)

FRIDAY, 9th MAY: 7 p.m.

CENTRAL HALL, WESTMINSTER

Admission Free   Collection

THOSE WOMEN AGAIN (left)

It showed a touching faith in society for the most respectable of women – civil servants and teachers – to take to the streets to win the public to their cause. Here, in 1955, the NAWCS joined with the NUWTs – the National Association of Women Civil Servants with the National Union of Women Teachers – to protest against the government's lack of action on the equal pay issue. The banners are less amateur than they look. 'Turkish Women' had equal pay already and 'Mr Gaitskell', the Labour Party leader at the time, was reminded that a general election was coming up.

A VARIETY OF CAUSES

There were demonstrations against America and Britain's involvement in the Korean war (top right), with women protesting as part of a Communist peace rally at Marble Arch in London in 1950. On Indian Independence Day, 15 August, a small group of Asians outside India House staged this protest against discrimination (top left). A warning of troubles to come

was caught in the Irish nationalist poster (above) pasted on a wall in Belfast in 1952. Ulster was not the only place that some desired to separate from Britain. These students outside the British embassy in Madrid (above left) are demanding its return to Spain. Known as 'Gib' or 'the Rock', the tiny island guarding the entrance to the Mediterranean was ceded to Britain in perpetuity in 1954.

up against ex-allies: they were with West Germany against former ally Russia. The cream of British front-line armour, and a large part of the RAF, were based there.

An extensive empire

British forces were still deployed in the Middle East and assured the security of the Gulf States. The sprawling camps in the Canal Zone of Egypt held great reservoirs of men and machines. There was a garrison in Aden in the Yemen, and a naval base from which the Royal Navy guarded the southern approach to the Suez Canal. The shipping lanes on the northern side of the canal were patrolled from its bases in Malta, Gibraltar and Cyprus.

There was a base at Simonstown in South Africa to protect the passage around the Cape, while the great naval dockyard at Singapore, and the presence in Hong Kong, projected British power into Asia. The RAF had airfields off the coast of Oman, at Gan in the Indian Ocean, in Cyprus and in Egypt. The huge base at Habbaniya in Iraq, a delighted RAF mechanic found, had 'swimming pools, theatres, churches, cinemas and every sport you can imagine'.

The empire itself, even though now shorn of India, the 'jewel in the crown', and reconstituted as the Commonwealth, was still the world's largest and the furthest flung. The dominions apart, the British were responsible for its security, too. This had traditionally involved British officers with local troops, but independence movements were putting extra strain on British resources, for British troops were needed in Cyprus and Kenya as well as Malaya.

This all needed manpower and uniforms were as common a sight as ever on trains and railway stations. (It was only with IRA terrorism two decades later that the armed forces ended the practice of wearing uniforms when travelling in public.) On 'Enlistment Thursdays', a great tide of conscripts passed through the British Railways network, heading for camps and barracks.

It was compulsory for every youth to register with the Ministry of Labour on his 18th birthday. That was followed within a fortnight by a medical. Non-attendance could be punished by two years in prison, but it rarely happened. The father, and often the mother, of most boys had been in uniform during the war. The tradition of service was strong. The number of 'conshies' (conscientious objectors) was tiny, never exceeding 0.4 per cent. For each sailor or marine, 12 conscripts went into the RAF and 33 became soldiers.

A few escaped this rite of passage, though only clergymen and the Northern Irish were exempt as of right – it was feared that any attempt to impose National

KOREA BOUND
Men of 55 Independent Squadron prepare to board ship at Southampton in 1950. The ship, the *Empire Windrush*, is better known for bringing the first West Indian immigrants to Britain in 1948, but these men are bound for Korea. War broke out after Communist North Korea invaded South Korea in June 1950. The Commonwealth forces, who numbered 14,000 at the end of the conflict, included Australians, New Zealanders, South Africans and Canadians as well as British. By the end of the conflict, in July 1953, they had lost 1078 killed.

NATIONAL SERVICE

YOU 'ORRIBLE LITTLE MEN

Conscription had been introduced during the war, but the government retained it in peacetime because of Britain's continuing global responsibilities, from keeping the peace in Germany to blocking Communist expansion in Asia. National Service became a rite of passage for the nation's young men. On 'Enlistment Thursdays' they headed off to camps and barracks for their basic training. One of the first rituals to happen to them when they got there was to be given an army hair cut.

Recruits to the East Yorkshire Regiment were issued with uniforms and boots from the camp stores (top). Then they were exposed to the tender mercies of drill sergeants, some of them equipped with boxing gloves (middle), and all with powerful lungs and sharp tongues. Arms drill was an important part of the training, and the lack of synchronisation displayed here (bottom) may already have provoked an outburst from the unseen drill instructor.

Service in Ulster could spark nationalist riots. In practice, miners, merchant seamen, fishermen (sea-going ones), farm workers, graduate science teachers and police cadets all enjoyed indefinite deferment. For the others, the grateful nation provided them with free rail warrants and 4 shillings as an advance on their pay.

Barrack life

Basic training provided a raw conscript with a three or four month introduction to service life, to the joys of No 3 Green Blanco for webbing and Brasso polish for buckles and cap badges. It was, as it were, a communal cold bath for the nation's young men. They were torn from home, stripped of their civilian clothes, most of their hair and all of their privacy, and flung together regardless of background. Some suffered agonies of shyness, like the young Alan Bennett who was used to praying: 'I lie there in my bed … as the blizzard of obscenity that has been going on all day gradually dwindles and my comrades fall asleep,' he wrote. 'I wonder if I were to get up in the dark and say my prayers whether anyone would notice.'

They lived in Barrack Spiders, wooden huts with a washing area and eight rooms, with 20 men to each room. They were woken at 5.30 or 6.00 am. After breakfast, they were assembled on the parade ground and put through their paces by a drill sergeant. Weapons training and fieldcraft followed until 5.00 pm. Seeking an evening's amusement or a drink outside camp in style was stymied by the meagre pay. National servicemen got £1 8 shillings (£1.40) a week in 1950, when average pay was £8 8s 6d. It was raised to £1 18s [£1.90] in 1960, but by that time the average wage had gone up to £15 10s.

By a typically British quirk, the privately educated were often the best equipped to deal with training. They were used to dormitories, compulsory runs, menial chores, beatings and cold baths, having survived all these at boarding school. Many had been in the school cadet force. Roger Cooper, a journalist later imprisoned and subjected to mock executions in an Iranian jail, said on his release that anyone who had been to British public school or done national service would find prison in Tehran 'a piece of cake'. Cooper had endured both in the 1950s.

Officer selection

The early egalitarianism of square-bashing, boot-shining and bed-making, under the eye and lashing tongue of fearsome NCOs, soon gave way to selection. The interview with the PSO, the Personnel Selection Officer, was a make-or-break affair, like the 'eleven plus' at school. Officer potential was based on pre-call up education and abilities shown in basic training. Those judged to have it went to a WOSBy – a War Office Selection Board – and then on to officer training at Eaton Hall in Cheshire or Mons Barracks in Aldershot.

A small elite, including Bennett and his fellow playwright Michael Frayn, were garnered for Russian interpreters' courses. They had a six-month course at Cambridge, taught by university staff, and lodged in officers' quarters. The skill

They were torn from home, stripped of their civilian clothes, most of their hair and all of their privacy, and flung together regardless of background.

was supposedly vital for the Cold War, but in what way was not always clear. 'I never did any interpreting, there was just translation of documents,' Frayn said later. 'They were all marked "secret" but they were actually mostly cuttings from Soviet newspapers. So in what way they were secret, only God knows.'

Sportsmen were well looked after. Rivalry between services and regiments was intense. Any decent cricketer, footballer or rugby player who made his unit's top team could expect to have a comfortable time. The best, like Bobby Charlton, played for the army. In a game played in November 1956 at Manchester's Maine Road stadium, the Army took on an FA team in front of a crowd of over 50,000. The Army XI had four Manchester United players, two each from Sheffield United and Spurs, and one from Liverpool: not surprisingly, they won 4-1.

The postings lottery

For the majority, postings after training were largely a matter of pot-luck. A lad could suffer the bleak dampness of potato-peeling in Catterick, the huge army camp in Yorkshire, or revel in the warmth and natural splendours of Kenya. He could be in comfortable barracks in Berlin, or in stifling conditions in the Canal Zone. One in twelve saw action. By 1951 men on National Service made

> ## Sportsmen were well looked after … The best, like Bobby Charlton, played for the army.

up half of the total British army manpower, and there was never a day in the Fifties when forces were not on active operations somewhere East of Suez, or, with Cyprus, in the Mediterranean. Between 1945 and the time the last man got his call-up papers in December 1960, a total of 395 national servicemen were killed in action.

The Glorious Glosters

To an extent, familiarity with war had bred public indifference. The distant fighting in Korea was noticed only when it flared up and the British were involved. The stand of the Glorious Glosters against the Chinese Red Army on the Imjin River in April 1951 was one battle that caught the imagination. The 750 men of the 1st Battalion were attacked by four divisions of at least 10,000 men, but they held out long enough to save the Allied line. Only 63 returned, and the regiment won two Victoria Crosses. By and large, though, despite 1078 British servicemen killed, Korea was a forgotten war; Britain seemed always to be at war, and this one was a long way away.

Two-way family favourites

Every Sunday lunchtime, a BBC radio request programme bought Britain's far-flung people together. Its introduction was one of the most familiar mantras of the decade. 'The time in Britain is twelve noon,' presenter Jean Metcalfe began. 'In Germany it's one o'clock, but home and away it's time for Two-Way Family Favourites.' The show put soldiers and families stationed abroad in touch with

THE JUNGLE EMERGENCY
'CTs', short for 'communist terrorists', were fighting to destabilise Malaya and open the door to Communist rule there. Sir Gerald Templer (above in 1952, with volunteers under training) was the High Commissioner and Commander in Chief in Malaya who frustrated and outfought them. The war was fought largely in remote jungles and plantations. Here (right), a soldier in the Royal West Kents burns a leech off a comrade's back on a jungle mission in 1953.

Postings after training were largely a matter of
pot-luck … from the bleak dampness of Catterick
to the warmth and natural splendours of Kenya.

relatives at home. It had a peak audience of 16 million in Britain, but it was listened to wherever forces' radio could be picked up. In fact, it could be three-way, or four-way, linking families in Germany, the Mediterranean, the Far East, Australia, Africa ...

The Festival of Britain

'This is no time for despondency,' said the King when he opened the Festival of Britain in May, a month after the Imjin battle. The Festival marked the centennial of the great 1851 Exhibition in Hyde Park, and it was an equally spectacular success, with 8.5 million visitors. The themes in 1951 were the exploration of sea, earth, sky and space – a reminder of how great a part the British had played in all of these. Towering over the site, like a strange spaceship, was an illuminated cigar tube of steel and aluminium called The Skylon. Wags compared it to the national economy, because it had no visible means of support.

Sculptures by Henry Moore, Barbara Hepworth and Lynn Chadwick added the exuberance and sophistication of art to the technology on display. Sir Roy Strong, former director of the Victoria & Albert Museum, would later call it 'the last really great stylistic statement this country made'. It was also the first evidence that austerity was over.

Some pavilions were for 'fun, fantasy and colour', and the restaurant tables and chairs in bright plastics with spindly legs and ball feet were a far cry from the

P-P-PICK UP A PENGUIN
In the 1950s these familiar sweets and chocolate biscuits were keen to stress their health benefits.

SHOPPING FOR SWEETS
To the delight of children across the country, sweets came off ration for good in February 1953, but even then the chocolate eclairs that this little girl is buying were a special treat. Most people had not yet seen a supermarket; the tradition of the local grocery, with personal service, was the standard of the day. Clouds were already gathering, though. The popular magazine *Picture Post* first ran this picture in a story called: 'The Shop round the Corner – Does It Deserve to Survive?'

'utility' furniture still in the shops. Upriver, the Festival Pleasure Gardens at Battersea Park featured a Fun Fair, a tree walk, fountains, a children's zoo, candy floss and ice cream. One child remembered it years later for a glass of milk, the first chilled drink she had ever had. More than 250 miles of Festival rock were sold. There were rides on the Emett Festival Railway, with engines like the Nellie and the Wild Goose based on the whimsical drawings of Rowland Emett, a cartoonist for *Punch*, the venerable comic weekly. Entrance to the Pleasure Gardens was two shillings, or a shilling on Sundays, when the Fun Fair was shut. Entertainment on the Sabbath was still frowned on in the metropolis, if not to the same degree as in the Scottish isles or Wales.

A Festival ship, the *Campania*, toured British ports, and a 'land travelling exhibition' took some of the highlights to the bigger provincial cities. Specially fitted-out Festival buses toured the Continent to enlighten the Europeans on Britain's scientific skills. When they had finished, they were put to work on the number 9 and 73 bus routes running out of Mortlake Garage in London. The Festival lifted people's spirits. When it closed in September, Archbishop Fisher said it had been 'a real family party' and a 'good thing for us all' – but it did not save the Labour government.

> '**It was a marvellous uplifting experience. We were young, the war was over, and there we were, full of hope, dancing on the South Bank. The breathtaking shapes and colours evoked a wonderful feeling of freedom.**'
>
> Jane Bown, photographer

TIME FOR CHANGE

Ernest Bevin, one of the greatest of all foreign secretaries, had died a month before the Festival opened. Over the summer, Attlee had become ill while Aneurin Bevan and Hugh Gaitskell fought as rivals for the leadership. Bevan resigned in fury when charges were imposed on dental and ophthalmic treatment as a way of meeting the escalating defence estimates for the Korean War. The government was fatigued and tetchy. It fell in the general election of October 1951. Winston Churchill was back as prime minister at the age of 77. It was the first time he had won an election as leader of the Conservative Party. His majority was only 16 seats, although this proved to be enough.

Churchill was, of course, an old Tory warhorse, and the government lost no time in getting rid of every trace of the 'socialist' festival. The pavilions were demolished, and even the plaster doves that had fluttered above the whimsical Lion and the Unicorn pavilion were auctioned off for a guinea apiece. Only the

continued on page 41

THE FESTIVAL OF BRITAIN

The Festival took place between May and September 1951 and was the first event of real flamboyance in Britain since the war. The main exhibition occupied 27 acres of cleared bomb sites on the South Bank of the Thames in central London. The scene was dominated by the Dome of Discovery, while further up-river – a threepenny boat-ride away – Battersea Park hosted the Festival Pleasure Gardens and Fun Fair. The London site was the main focus of the Festival, but events took place all over Britain, from street parties to singing contests.

THE FESTIVAL SITE
This view of the Thames in 1951 shows the Dome of Discovery in the foreground, just upriver from the Hungerford Bridge carrying the railway line into Charing Cross Station. The Skylon – a giant, skyward-pointing steel and aluminium tube – is visible between the bridge and the Dome. The Royal Festival Hall and Shot Tower stand between the Hungerford and Waterloo bridges. The Festival had two piers, the Nelson and Rooney, and regular boats ferried visitors upriver to the Festival Pleasure Gardens at Battersea Park.

FLYING FIRST
The Saunders-Roe A1 was the world's first – and almost last – jet flying-boat fighter. It was towed up the Thames to the festival site.

'A palace in thunderland, sizzling with scientific witches' brew.'

Dylan Thomas, poet

A FUN FAMILY DAY OUT
A woman studies her Festival souvenir programme and guide, deciding what to see next. It cost 4 shillings to get into the festival at the turnstiles, with children half price. The Dome of Discovery at the heart of the activities bore an uncanny resemblance to the Millennium Dome in Greenwich today, but this one was taken to heart by its 8.5 million visitors.

DEFYING GRAVITY
A young woman has difficulty maintaining her modesty on a ride at the Battersea Fun Fair – the rapid spin kept the riders firmly stuck to the wall, but did not do the same for her skirt. The fair at Battersea had a water splash, a Looper, a Caterpillar Ride and much more.

LOTS TO LOOK AT
The exhibition drew visitors from all walks of life, with something for everyone. Some pavilions were for 'fun, fantasy and colour'. There were dazzling displays of crystallography, cybernetics and aeronautics.

NEW VIEW
The audience in the 'Telecinema' were equipped with special goggles to watch the newly invented 'stereoscopic' films, that are better known today as 3-D.

THE ELECTION: OCTOBER 1951

WINNIE'S BACK
Winston Churchill salutes his supporters on his victory in the October 1951 general election. His wife, Clementine, is by his side, looking absolutely delighted. He won by just 16 seats. One Conservative who was not successful in the election was Margaret Thatcher, shown here canvassing a local chimney sweep. Her chances of success were not great – it was her second election contest in the safe Labour seat of Dartford. She eventually won a seat, in Finchley, in 1959, several years after Churchill had resigned and handed over the prime ministership to Anthony Eden.

THE TORY TEAM

WINSTON CHURCHILL
Leader of the Conservative and Unionist Party

Cut out Government waste

VOTE CONSERVATIVE

Turn hopes into Homes

VOTE CONSERVATIVE

CHURCHILL COMMIT ROOMS

Royal Festival Hall remained. But Churchill was a man of many parts, an aristocrat who remained proudly 'Mr Churchill', at various times a soldier, journalist, water-colourist, prolific and Nobel prize-winning author, builder of brick walls for relaxation in his country house at Chartwell.

His government followed the consensus politics of 'Butskellism', half Tory left, as personified by the new Chancellor, R A Butler, and half Labour right, as in the public-school educated Hugh Gaitskell. The Tories promised lower taxes, less bureaucracy and red tape – 'Set the people free' was their campaign slogan – and a massive new house-building programme. Only iron and steel were denationalised. Coal and the railways, the big loss makers, remained with the State.

Easier times ahead

It was a good time to come to power. A feel-good factor would boost the Tories as rationing was steadily abolished. Tea went off-ration in 1952. Sweets went off in February 1953, and, to the relief of children across the country, stayed off. That September, sugar was de-rationed, and the average Briton was then free to indulge, soon making Britain the world's fifth largest sugar consumer, after the likes of Greenlanders and Icelanders.

The miracle year was 1954. Butter, margarine, cooking fat and cheese went in a rush, and finally, in July, bacon and meat came off. Rationing was over. It marked a watershed. 'Almost at once, affluence came hurrying on the heels of

COKE LIGHT
Some coke was already available above the ration in 1953. That was when the gatekeeper at the Nine Elms Gas Depot in London (above) gave this young woman two bags in return for a chit. But even the 'off ration' fuel was itself rationed to two bags per person. It was not until the following year that restrictions on fuel were lifted.

penury,' wrote the social historian Harry Hopkins. 'Suddenly the shops were piled high with all sorts of goods. Boom was in the air.'

The Tories were the low tax party, and they delivered. The government was taking 35 per cent of the national product in taxes and social security contributions when they came to power. That was down to 27 per cent by 1958. As a result, people had more money to spend. Fortunately, the food shops also had more to sell. Food shopping still entailed separate visits to butchers, bakers, fruit and vegetable merchants, fishmongers and grocers. The first real supermarket was opened by Sainsbury's in Croydon in June 1950, advertising 'Q-less shopping' and self-service with a wide range of goods. The writing was on the wall for small shopkeepers, but their decline was to be relatively slow. By the end of the 1950s, there were still only 367 supermarkets in the whole country.

> ## 'Almost at once, affluence came hurrying on the heels of penury. Suddenly shops were piled high with all sorts of goods. Boom was in the air.'
>
> Harry Hopkins, social historian

An unenviable food reputation

Dining out was a luxury in 1950 – in terms of cost, if not cuisine. On the menu were brown soup, overcooked Argentinian meat and stewed vegetables with boiling gravy, followed by tinned Australian peaches with ersatz cream. The meal was usually eaten in an overheated hotel dining room, and washed down with a wine of dubious provenance and worse taste. The food critic Egon Ronay described food in Wales as 'gastronomic rape'. But there was a glimmer of hope. In 1951, Raymond Postgate brought out his *Good Food Guide* to restaurants in Britain. Postgate was a curious figure, the son of a classics professor, a 'conshie' in the First World War, a writer of detective stories, and a founder member of the British Communist Party, who then devoted himself to the much-needed improvement of British cuisine.

Tastes in food were beginning, slowly, to change. In the better-off homes, Elizabeth David ruled. After studying in France, David had lived on a Greek island

THE WORKING LUNCH
City gents enjoy lunch at the bar, washed down with a pint of real ale pulled from the hand pumps. A few took long and elaborate lunches, but quickly eaten meals in pubs were more common. The pace of life in the financial markets was accelerating. Recurrent sterling crises led to tight restrictions – there was a £50 limit on the amount that a person could take abroad – and feverish dealings in the foreign exchange markets.

MAKES COOKING SO EASY

My mother said
I never should
Miss my Guinness
—As if I would!

A GUINNESS
A DAY IS
GOOD FOR YOU

REBIRTH OF ADVERTISING
Two colour posters from the 1950s
advertising household brands that
are still going strong today.

and in Cairo, before returning to the bleak British table. Her *Mediterranean Cooking*, published in 1950, was the beginning of a little revolution in home cooking. Her aim, she said, was 'to bring a flavour of those blessed lands of sun and sea and olive trees into … English kitchens'.

The next year, David revealed the simple secrets of *French Country Cooking*, and in 1954 paid homage to *Italian Food*. As the ingredients she loved gradually became available – aubergines, garlic, peppers, courgettes, fine hams and salamis, 'not mass produced Milanese or squalid Danish' – her best-selling books changed from tantalising descriptions of the unattainable into actual dishes on dining tables. By 1955, she already found things so 'startlingly different' that there was hardly a food she mentioned that could not be bought somewhere, 'even if it is one or two shops'.

Of coffee bars and fast food

David was a middle-class adult phenomenon. The young were far more influenced by American food. Lyons, familiar in every fair-sized town for their Corner Houses, opened the first Wimpy Bar in 1954. The name came from the Popeye cartoon character J Wellington Wimpy, and the brand had started in Chicago before the war. A Wimpy burger cost 2 shillings (10p), or 3s 9d (18.5p) for a King Size. There were frankfurters, too, and American fruit pie, Whippy milk shakes and Tastee-Freeze desserts.

Wimpy Bars were phenomenally successful, a sign both of admiration of things American and of increasing teenage purchasing power. In the glory days, before the arrival of MacDonald's, there were more than a thousand Wimpys around the country – there were nine on London's Oxford Street alone – and the charms of the trademark ketchup bottle, in the form of a big red plastic tomato, were admired in 23 foreign countries as well, from South America to the Middle East. The American roadside diner, meanwhile, inspired the caravan-maker Sam Alper to open the first Little Chef restaurant in Reading in 1958. It was to become the largest roadside chain in the country.

What wasn't American in catering tended to be Italian. The number of Italians living in Britain doubled over the decade. In 1955 Frank and Aldo Berni founded their eponymous steak chain, which grew from a base in the West Country. The first Berni Inn was a converted Bristol coaching inn, The Rummer, draped in heavy red velvet, soon aromatic with cigarette smoke. The menu was small, in content and in price, but had little in common with menus in Italian restaurants. Most diners kicked off with a medium sherry and splashed out 8 shillings for three courses consisting of prawn cocktail, followed by steak, chips and peas, with Black Forest gateau for dessert. Trained chefs – like tablecloths, replaced by

A FAMILY FAREWELL
Although it looks as though the royal family are just arriving, in fact they have not been away. King George with Queen Elizabeth and younger daughter Princess Margaret are leaving the plane that is about to take Princess Elizabeth and Prince Philip to Kenya on holiday. It was the last time that Elizabeth saw her father. She would return to Britain as Queen Elizabeth II.

A TRIPLE TRAIN CRASH
This is the scene on 8 October, 1952, after the worst peacetime train crash in Britain. It was a double collision involving three trains. A local passenger train was in Harrow and Wealdstone station when it was hit in the rear by the express sleeper from Perth in Scotland. An express from London bound for Liverpool and Manchester ploughed into the wreckage. The driver and fireman of the sleeper had passed two signals at danger. Why is not known, for they were both killed.

place mats – were redundant in the Berni Inn. The steak was bought in ready to cook and a deep fryer and grill were the only kitchen essentials.

Other Italians brought coffee and the Espresso bar with them. The Gaggia machine was the key: it used high-pressure steam and freshly ground beans to make a strong, vibrant coffee that seemed to come from a wholly different plant to the weak sludge served in British restaurants. The Moka bar in London's Soho was the first to import a Gaggia in 1952. From there, they spread rapidly across the country, breaking through the 1000 mark six years later. The British-Italian coffee bar was a far cry from the classic cafés of Paris or Milan. It had Formica counters, plastic tables, Apfelstrudel and rubber plants, but it also had a jukebox, which for its young customers made it the place to be.

Birth of the EU

In July, the European Coal and Steel Community was launched with six founding members – France, West Germany, Italy, Belgium, the Netherlands and Luxembourg. Britain was left out of what would soon become the Brussels-based European Economic Community, still without Britain, that was to strengthen the political ties at the heart of the Continent.

A RUN OF DISASTERS

The King, loved for his slight stammer, shyness and fortitude during the war, died on 6 February, 1952. He was only 56. Princess Elizabeth was on holiday with Prince Philip in Kenya. She flew back to Heathrow as Queen Elizabeth II. The next month, Churchill made the sombre announcement that Britain had the atomic bomb and had thus become the world's third nuclear power, after the United States and the Soviet Union. Tales of 'flying saucers', meanwhile, crossed the Atlantic, where Washington was said to have been buzzed by sinister Unidentified Flying Objects; the UFO craze was launched.

continued on page 51

THE DEATH OF KING GEORGE

'For fifteen years George VI was King. Never at any moment in all the perplexities at home and abroad, in public or in private, did he fail in his duties. Well does he deserve the farewell salute of all his governments and peoples ...'

Winston Churchill, in his eulogy for the King

A KING, HUSBAND AND FATHER
The coffin with the body of George VI
arrives at King's Cross (above), London,
from Sandringham on 11 February, 1952.
The Queen Mother, with the new Queen
Elizabeth and Princess Margaret, travelled
to Buckingham Palace the same day (right).
Crowds waited patiently to pay their last
respects as the King lay in state in
Westminster Abbey, before he was laid to
rest at St George's Chapel, Windsor.

A 'LONDON PARTICULAR'

That was the phrase that Dickens coined for London fog in *Bleak House*. It was indeed synonymous with London and famous around the world, as a song, as a type of raincoat, as a background to the tales of Sherlock Holmes. The locals called it 'smog', a foul and dangerous combination of smoke and fog, rich in acids and particles of soot. It was so thick that the conductor of the bus (left) had to walk in front of his vehicle to guide the driver on a December evening in 1952. The mortality rate from bronchitis and pneumonia was up seven-fold that month. Deaths in London normally ran at about 250 a day, but they hit 900 a day. These clerical workers in the City of London (right) equipped themselves with smog masks before setting off to work. The 1952 smog prompted the Clean Air Act of 1956. This designated areas where only smokeless fuel could be burnt, and relocated power stations out of the cities and into the countryside.

Disaster strikes – and strikes again

In August 1952, floodwaters devastated the picturesque resort of Lynmouth in north Devon after 9 inches (230mm) of rain fell overnight on nearby Exmoor; 34 people died. Then, on 6 September, tragedy struck the Farnborough Air Show. Britain was a world leader in design and aircraft manufacture – it had recently built the Comet, the world's first jet passenger plane, as well as the Brabazon, the largest passenger airliner. A nuclear strike aircraft, the brand-new Vulcan V-bomber, was to fly at the show, along with a Javelin heavy fighter, a Britannia turbo-prop airliner, the Princess flying boat, plus various prototypes, all British-built and powered by British engines.

Thousands watched test pilot John Derry take off for his display flight in a twin-engined DH 110 fighter. He had been the first British pilot to break the sound barrier, exactly four years before. But as he went supersonic this time, the crowd saw the aircraft break up and then hurtle down towards them. One engine went over a hill on which many were standing and crashed into the car park behind it. The other ploughed directly into the crowd. Thirty-one people were killed, including Derry. There was no panic – an eyewitness spoke of the crowd 'parting like the Red Sea' as the ambulances arrived. Then after a short

THE AFTERMATH
A wrecked car is just part of the debris left on the beach by the flood that devastated Lynmouth on 16 August 1952. Lynmouth had seen floods before, but never like this. After the West Lyn burst its banks, a raging torrent swept down the village high street, bringing with it thousands of tons of rocks and anything else that stood in its path. A whole row of riverside cottages collapsed like a pack of cards and was washed away. The occupants were among the 34 people who died.

break, test pilot Neville Duke did a supersonic dive in a prototype Hawker Hunter, an aircraft that would later hold the world air speed record. It was his tribute to his fallen friend and to the crowd. An American boy, his mother hysterical, spoke in awe of 'British stoicism'. The upper lip was still definitely stiff.

The next month, three trains collided at Harrow and Wealdstone Station. The Perth-to-London express ran into the back of a commuter train travelling to London from Tring in Hertfordshire. Seconds later a third train, heading out of London, plunged into the wreckage. The crash was one of the worst in Britain's history, leaving 112 dead and nearly 340 injured.

Just as it seemed the year could not get worse, it did. Smog was not unusual in towns and cities in the 1950s, a result of coal fires and foggy weather conditions. But London was notorious. A particularly poisonous smog began there on 5 December, during a cold spell that had fires burning in grates and stoves in almost every house. By 8 December people in balcony seats at the Royal Festival Hall could not see the stage. Concentrations were eleven times worse than usual. The smog drifted everywhere, into hospital wards and nurseries, killing the elderly and sick. Over four days, some 4000 deaths were directly linked to the noxious fumes – a more severe rate of death, if for a briefer period, than in the great cholera epidemic of 1866. The episode was one of the key triggers that led to government action on pollution. A Clean Air Act was passed in 1956 and the pea-souper was eventually restricted to Sherlock Holmes films and folk memory.

A killer sea

Tragedy crept into the New Year. At the end of January, violent gales and an unusually high tide combined to drive the North Sea inland in a devastating storm surge. The floods hit the east coast at night, without warning. Some managed to escape the floodwaters by scrambling, in pitch dark, onto the roofs of their houses, but 307 people drowned in the worst peacetime disaster of 20th-century Britain. The same surge killed 1835 people in the Netherlands, especially low-lying Zeeland, and a further 132 were lost to the same storm when the ferry *Princess Victoria* foundered in the Irish Sea.

THE GREAT NORTH SEA FLOOD
High spring tides and severe gales produced a tidal surge in the North Sea at the beginning of February 1953. In places, the water level rose 5.6m (over 18ft) above normal. The tide and the giant waves overwhelmed sea defences. Worst affected was the Netherlands, but eastern England was badly hit, too. Canvey Island in the Thames Estuary was one of the areas inundated. Most of the 58 who died there were in bungalows in the eastern part of the island; the water reached ceiling height, trapping and drowning the people inside. Here, Canvey islanders try to salvage some of their possessions (left), while residents from The Avenue are evacuated by rowing boat (right).

A NEW ELIZABETHAN ERA

The year 1953 was a vintage one, its triumphs and joys made the merrier by the sadnesses of the year before.

CORONATION CELEBRATION Up and down the land, children enjoyed street parties on the Queen's big day.

CONQUEST AND CORONATION

Then, life suddenly lightened. The 'Matthews Cup Final' was played on 2 May, 1953. The legendary Stanley Matthews, a dazzling winger in baggy shorts, was 38 and had never won an FA Cup winner's medal. His side, Blackpool, were 3-1 down in the final against Bolton Wanderers with just 20 minutes to go, and it looked as though he never would win one. Then Matthews passed to Stan Mortensen, Blackpool's centre forward, who scored. Mortensen scored again with a free kick. With less than 60 seconds to go, Matthews made one of his bewitching runs up the wing and gave the perfect pass to Bill Perry, who scored the winning goal. Blackpool won 4–3.

Sentimentalists were further delighted when Gordon Richards, the best-loved jockey in a horseracing-mad country, won the Derby at his 28th time of asking. Even the Ashes went right. They returned to England, after 19 years with Australia, on the fourth day of the fifth Test at the Oval. The bluff Yorkshireman Len Hutton was the first professional player to captain the England side. The winning run was scored by Denis Compton.

Slim sporting rewards

Compton was perhaps the first sporting hero to be a pin-up boy and marketing man's dreamboat. The trend has grown familiar since, although Compton's achievement in playing on the Arsenal wing and winning an FA Cup winner's medal in 1950, as well as enchanting cricket spectators as a peerless batsman at Lords, will surely never be repeated. He was one of the last men to combine mastery of both the summer and winter games. He became the face of Brylcreem and was seen on roadsides, on buses and in newspapers across the nation. What astonished Neville Cardus, the much-loved cricket correspondent of the *Manchester Guardian*, was that he was selected to advertise a hair product. 'Denis's hair', Cardus wrote, 'was unruly beyond the pacifying power of any cream, oil or unguent whatsoever.'

He could never have made his Brylcreem money with Arsenal. The maximum wage for footballers was fixed at the level of a skilled artisan. Not for nothing was Tom (later Sir Tom) Finney known as 'the Preston plumber'. He earned £20 a week from Preston North End during the season, and £17 over the summer. He topped this up with £50 for international appearances with England, and every five years he was entitled to a £500 benefit from his club. Finney played his last game in the First Division (the equivalent of today's Premiership) in the 1959–60 season. The wage limit was scrapped the next year, thanks to pressure from Jimmy Hill, the square-jawed future presenter of 'Match of the Day'.

Finney was perhaps the best all-round player England has produced. 'He would have been great in any team, in any match and in any year,' said Bill Shankly. 'Even if he'd been wearing an overcoat.' Absurdly, Finney would have been better off playing for a non-League side, where the maximum did not apply. But he had no bitterness. 'I would have loved to earn more, but I also believe that football treated Tom Finney well.'

ON TOP OF THE WORLD
The news that a British expedition had conquered Everest sent spirits soaring when it came through for Coronation Day in June 1953. The first men to stand on the world's highest summit were, in fact, the New Zealander Edmund Hillary and a Nepalese Sherpa, Tenzing Norgay (right). But the mountain had been named for a British surveyor, Sir George Everest. The first attempts to climb it were British, and every schoolboy knew of the fate of Mallory and Irvine, who had disappeared going for the summit in 1924. It was a British pilot who had first flown over it, a perilous achievement in an aircraft with an open cockpit, and the successful 1953 expedition was led by a British army officer, John Hunt. So it counted as a home victory.

THE PEOPLE'S GAME

THE PEOPLE'S PLAYER

In the days before 'Big Money' changed the game beyond measure, it was still possible for a small club with a fine tradition to win the FA Cup. In 1953, Blackpool beat Bolton Wanderers in the Final at Wembley. The as-yet uncrowned Queen presented the trophy and medals, and is seen here congratulating Stanley Matthews for his brilliant efforts in bringing the Seasiders back from the dead at 3-1 down to win 4-3 a heartbeat before the final whistle. 'The Cup' – and in the 1950s that phrase meant the FA Cup and no other – was lovingly polished (below) by Fred Packham before presentation to the winning captain. It was probably the most valued sporting trophy in England. The crowds attending matches in pre-television days (below) were far greater than today. The club marketing men had not yet got at them: there are no team shirts or club scarves on display in this queue, just sensible raincoats and hats.

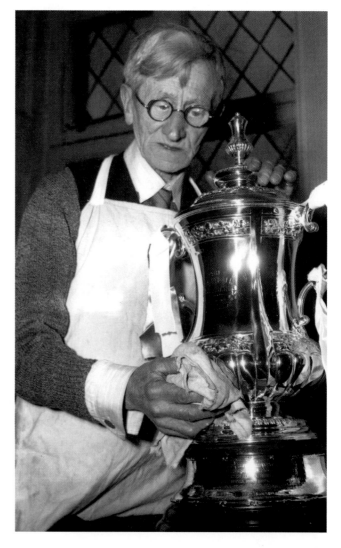

Crowning glory

That innocence and enthusiasm was reflected in the great event of the year: the coronation. It was fixed for 3 June – statistically the sunniest day of the year. In the event, it poured, but the crowds were happy for dramatic news had just come through from Nepal. The British expedition had made the first ascent of the world's highest mountain. After so many epic failures, Everest had been climbed. It mattered not a jot that the two who reached the top were a New Zealander, Edmund Hillary, and a Nepalese sherpa, Tenzing Norgay. The expedition was British mounted and led by John Hunt, and that was good enough. Since Mallory and Irvine had disappeared into the mists below the summit in 1924, still climbing strongly, the British had an almost proprietary interest in the mountain. The coincidence of conquest and coronation seemed to get the 'new Elizabethan age' off to a flying start.

The ceremony at Westminster Abbey was televised, which proved to be the making of the fledgling television industry – and of the first television dynasty, the Dimblebys. At the beginning of the year, there were fewer than 2 million TV sets in the country. A set cost £80, around eight times the average weekly wage, and many places had no coverage. Once the decision to transmit the coronation was made, though, the BBC set about putting up temporary transmitters. By the time of the great day, more than half-a-million more sets had been sold.

An audience of 20 million watched the fuzzy black and white pictures, listening to Richard Dimbleby's marathon 13-hour commentary. 'The moment of the Queen's crowning is come,' he intoned at its high point, becoming as it were the nation's commentator-in-chief, or 'Gold Microphone-in-Waiting' as the writer and wit Malcolm Muggeridge put it. The post would later be occupied by Richard's sons, David and Jonathan.

The televised ceremony cemented, too, the young Queen in the affections of the people – and in the global consciousness, as millions more people watched or listened overseas. The sight of young Prince Charles, looking awestruck in the Abbey at his mother in her regalia, gave a family feeling to the day. An estimated 3 million people lined the streets of London trying to catch a glimpse of Queen Elizabeth as she was driven by coach to Westminster Abbey and back to Buckingham Palace. Despite the damp day, a fly-past by the RAF down the Mall and a fireworks display marked the occasion. In the evening, the cheering crowd drew the Queen to the balcony of the palace no fewer than six times, while the crowds danced in Trafalgar Square and at street parties across the country.

Family values

The coronation was a renewal of the country's pride and stability. And despite its problems, 1950s Britain was a very secure and stable place. Its morality can seem quaint now. Two-Way Family Favourites, for example, had started out as Forces Favourites during the war and was mildly risqué whilst the fighting was going on. Now, it was studiously and morally a family show, stripped of references to girl

> The coronation was a renewal of the country's pride and stability.

continued on page 63

THE CORONATION

THE BIG DAY

It rained hard on 2 June, 1953, and the crowds got very wet. Nobody minded, except perhaps the grumpy looking peer (right) as he lifts up his robe to keep it dry on his way to the ceremony. A radiant young monarch arrived at Westminster Abbey wearing her coronation robes and Sovereign crown, with the Duke of Edinburgh and her Maids of Honour around her. There were not enough coachmen to take the many dignitaries to the Abbey, so country squires and farmers offered their services, and dressed up in Palace livery to drive the horse-drawn carriages. As 8000 guests looked on, the Queen was given the four symbols of authority: the orb and sceptre, the rod of mercy and the royal ring of rubies and sapphires. The Archbishop of Canterbury, Dr Geoffrey Fisher, then put St Edward's Crown on her head. Twenty million watched on new-fangled television sets and radio broadcasts went out in 44 languages. There were street parties the length and breadth of the country. The smiles of the ladies of Morpeth Street in London's East End (below) capture the mood of the day. 'Throughout all my life, and with all my heart', the Queen said in her message to the people, 'I shall strive to be worthy of your trust.' Few such promises have been kept more loyally or for longer than hers.

KIDS' CRAZES

In the pre-video-game age, the bits of kit most valued by children were low-tech and mechanical. The pogo stick (above), a strange contraption, a sort of hopping single stilt, was one of them. The fearless young operative bounced forward, rather like a kangaroo, though without the same grace and forward speed. They were said to have been invented by a Burmese farmer for his daughter, who was called Pogo. Whatever the truth of that, the design was patented by one George Hansburg in America in 1919. These 1950s children were in time to benefit from a recent breakthrough in design, the 'Master Pogo' with a stronger spring. Cowboys and Indians was an undying favourite. The Davy Crockett coonskin hat (left) was a must-have for Christmas.

friends and even fiancées. Jean Metcalfe, the show's presenter, met the future TV presenter Cliff Michelmore when he was the programme's link in Hamburg. Not a word of their romance appeared until they were safely married and he had left the programme.

After a post-war hiccup, when hasty wartime marriages were breaking up, the divorce rate fell back to around 2 to 3 per cent. Illegitimacy, which had crept up to 5 per cent at the end of the war, also dropped. Divorce carried a distinct social stigma. Adultery damaged careers – and ended some.

Child's play

Children entertained themselves with hopscotch, leapfrog, marbles, conkers, Cowboys and Indians. Boys joined the Ian Allen Locospotters Club, entered the 'Spotters of the Month' competition, and went trainspotting to Crewe or Clapham Junction. The hugely popular I-Spy books encouraged children to spot birds, animals, cars, aircraft. The I-Spy Tribe was run by a retired headmaster, Charles Warrell, the Big Chief I-Spy. At its height, it had half a million members.

Other worthy institutions for children included the Brownies, Cubs, Girl Guides, Boy Scouts and Boys Brigades, which between them had more than 2 million members in the Fifties. The Scouts Bob-a-Job Week was a regular fixture in the nation's calendar. There was a craze for badges and awards, and

A MULTI-RACIAL FUTURE
A mixed group of children pictured in the streets of Liverpool in 1954. The great city on the Mersey had been the first stopping point for huge numbers of Irish immigrants for more than a century. As a seaport, it had long had a coloured population. In the early 1950s, it was one of the first British cities to see a large multi-ethnic influx, not just of West Indians, but also Chinese, Indians, Pakistanis and Africans. This process, which was to change Britain's previously homogenous society, was now beginning to gather pace.

BECOMING A BOBBY
The British bobby, in his unmistakable helmet, was as famous round the world as the London bus. So was his headquarters. This recruiting poster urges young men to write to New SCOTLAND YARD, London. That was address enough.

MATCH OF THE DAY
Playing football in the street (below) was safe: partly because traffic was rare, especially in poor areas, and partly because there was so little casual violence and general nastiness. The 1950s was often a dingy world, but a child's imagination could turn the asphalt and paving stones into the green grass of Wembley, without his mother having to worry about him.

for Davy Crockett imitation coonskin hats and buckskin suits, priced at 12/6d and £2 9s 11d respectively. Enid Blyton books of *The Famous Five* and *The Secret Seven* were popular with both boys and girls, as was Arthur Ransome's *Swallows and Amazons* and the character-building tales of G A Henty. Boys devoured *Eagle* comics by the score, featuring Dan Dare, 'pilot of the future', and the investigator Harris Tweed. Dennis the Menace lurked mischievously in the *Beano*. Roy of the Rovers outdid the footballing feats of Stanley Matthews in *Tiger*.

LAW-ABIDING LAND

Crime was rare in 1950s Britain. Drugs were almost unknown. From an absolute low in 1935, when the country was historically at its most law-abiding, there had been a sharp rise in recorded offences during the war, up by 56 per cent. This was blamed on the blackout and the presence of so many foreign troops and troops on leave, who knew there was little chance of being caught. The crime rate fell after the war and between 1950 and 1955 it fell again, by more than 5 per cent.

It was not Utopia. Violence was up, with twice as many crimes against the person and three times as many rapes in 1951 as in the last full pre-war year. But looking back, compared to what was to come, it seemed so. From 1955, the rate began climbing again, slowly but inexorably, towards its present heights.

Crime statistics are notoriously easy to fudge. Nonetheless, the evidence of a law-abiding society was physically obvious. There were few no-go areas. Relations between police and public were in general warm. The actor Jack Warner began a long-running television soap, *Dixon of Dock Green*, in 1956. It was as deeply embedded in the national soul as *Coronation Street*, attracting regular audiences of 14 million, drawing on the same wellsprings of nostalgia and familiarity. The theme song, 'Just an Ordinary Copper', caught the programme's essence – the genial and avuncular PC Dixon maintained law and order in his patch over 434 episodes, with no more than a seldom drawn truncheon. 'Evenin' all' he said at the start of each episode, with a reassuring touch of his helmet.

The bicycle-riding Dixon and the petty crooks he pursued were a world away from the cynical, savvy police in the tyre-squealing *Z-Cars* and the hardened villains they pursued at the start of the 1960s. But the gentler society Dixon came from had substance in the Fifties. In close-knit communities in towns and cities up and down the land, neighbours looked out for each other. People often did not bother to lock the front door to

INFAMOUS NAMES IN CRIME

MULTIPLE MURDER

John Christie is driven away from court inside a police van during his trial for murdering his wife Ethel at 10 Rillington Place in London's Notting Hill. He was later convicted of six murders, including that of his wife, and was hanged in 1953. Three years earlier, the bodies of the wife and baby daughter of another tenant, Timothy Evans, had been found at Rillington Place. Christie had been a chief witness for the prosecution at Evans's trial. Evans was found guilty of the murder of his daughter, and had been hanged. The discovery of other bodies at the house, murdered by Christie, threw doubt on the Evans verdict and was a key factor in the campaign to abolish capital punishment.

TERRIBLE TWINS

Reggie (on the left) and Ronnie Kray pose with their mother Violet as up-and-coming 17-year-old amateur boxers in 1950. They were particularly close to their mother. Their father had deserted them and the army, and had gone on the run. The twins were to become notorious professional gangsters in the East End of London, mixing with fashionable figures who found it exciting to be seen hobnobbing with 'real' criminals. The murder of a minor member of their gang, Jack 'the Hat' McVitie, in 1967 was to prove their downfall. Ronnie, the more dominant of the two, was certified insane while in prison.

their house when they went out or to bed. In the country, drivers left keys in the car after they parked it in the garage. Guards on trains and bus conductors were entrusted with keeping an eye out for young children, to make sure that they got off at the right stop.

Town children played in the streets without adult supervision. A walk round the back streets of any industrial town would reveal girls skipping with washing lines and playing hopscotch, boys leap-frogging and belting a football, making do with discarded pullovers for goalposts. Street cricket was a reason why it was still truly an English national game. Whether or not the local school had a playing field, a child needed no more than a few friends, some chalk to draw stumps on a brick wall, a bat and a ball, and in his mind's eye he could be walking out at Lords to open the batting.

War on want

Poverty had not been eradicated in post-war Britain, though some, like Seebohm Rowntree, believed that it almost had. The philanthropist and chocolate manufacturer made a study of the poorest areas of York, and reported in 1950 that the number of people living in poverty in the city had fallen from 18 per cent in 1936 to just 1.5 per cent in 1950. *The Times* ran an editorial claiming that Britain had recorded a 'remarkable' achievement: 'no less than the virtual abolition of the sheerest want'.

FAR FROM THE CROWD
The rhythms of the countryside were still those of centuries gone by, especially in more remote rural areas. This harvest scene was recorded on the island of Lewis and Harris in the Outer Hebrides in 1955. The swing of the scythe was the image of Father Time himself, an unbroken link to the pre-combine harvester age, when farms that were soon to be worked by just a couple of men employed ten or more. The skill of the shepherd (above right) was less easy for machines to imitate, but sheep farmers faced tough competition from Australian and New Zealand lamb and wool. Far from the 'all mod cons' of new city housing, running water has not yet reached the individual cottages in Glencoe Village in Scotland (right). But the telephone has.

It was true that the welfare reforms had provided health care and a social safety net. Housing, though, was still in crisis. The ravages of the Blitz were evident in the bomb sites that littered the big cities, some in use as car parks, most overgrown with weeds and bushes. The industrial slums remained home to thousands – rows of back to backs, two rooms up and two down, with shared outdoor privies. Amid the sour smells of gasworks and factory chimneys, and the scum-cold and abandoned canals, terraced streets echoed to the haunting noise of the whistles of shunting engines, and the time kept by harsh factory hooters. It was the world of 'dog muck, cigarette packets, old ashes', described by Richard Hoggart in *The Uses of Literacy*, his book on working class culture. Hoggart himself escaped from it in Leeds by getting a grammar school scholarship.

The country life

The country was another world, encapsulated for predominantly urban listeners on BBC radio's *The Archers*, first transmitted in 1950. Children went nutting and rosehip-picking, gathered wild flowers and helped with the harvest. Mechanisation was steadily reducing the numbers of those who made a living from the land, but there were still about 1.4 million employed in agriculture, compared with just 200,000 today. The farm labourer, in collarless shirt, belt and braces, remained the predominant figure of the countryside. Carthorses had not yet been completely ousted by tractors and were a common sight. Hay and wheat were cut by scythe and turned by hand-rake in the awkward, patchwork fields of smaller farms;

milking was often still by hand. Labourers lived in tied cottages, farmhouses were for farmers, by and large, and a vicar still lived in the vicarage. Rural Britain, even close to the big cities, was still much the same society that it had long been.

Change was afoot, however, in the management of flora and fauna. An Agriculture Act, aimed at boosting food production, gave subsidies for insecticides like DDT and chemical weed killers, with disastrous results for wildlife. Birds at the top of the food chain were most affected. Peregrines and sparrowhawks that feasted on pesticide-rich pigeons became rarer and rarer. Flowers disappeared from meadows. In 1954, an outbreak of myxomatosis almost wiped out rabbits.

AFRICAN PRIVILEGE
Aircraft were making it possible for these boys (above) to have the best of both worlds – term times at leading boarding schools in England, and holidays with their families among the farms and game-filled nature reserves of Kenya. The elegance and sheer Britishness of Lady Hamilton and her labrador (below), both distinguished 'settlers' in the colony, is matched by the formal dignity of the Africans in this colourful study of colonial life.

A CHANGING POPULATION

Britain was still a country of emigrants. The 'ten-pound Poms' continued to flow out to Australia, many sailed to Canada and New Zealand, and the annual flow to the United States reached 20,000. These were traditional destinations. The two Rhodesias – Northern and Southern, today's Zambia and Zimbabwe – were new. In the decade to 1955, the white population of Southern Rhodesia went from 80,000 to 200,000. In copper-rich Northern Rhodesia, it shot up twelve-fold.

It was among inbound immigrants rather than the outbound, though, where the scale began noticeably to change in the 1950s. Since the 18th century, small

PARADISE LOST
Troops from the Devonshire Regiment (above) march with kitbags and weapons before being posted to Kenya in 1955. A rebellion, drawing mainly on members of the Kikuyu tribe, had broken out three years before. The rebels were called 'Mau Mau', a word whose derivation remains uncertain, but their aim was clear – independence. In their campaign, the Mau Mau attacked white-owned farms and farmers, killing settlers and Kikuyu who remained loyal to the colonial regime. Militarily, they were never a serious threat. Politically, though, they drove a wedge between settlers and Whitehall, and ultimately gained independence for their country.

black communities had settled near seaports in places like Cardiff's Tiger Bay and Bootle in Liverpool. The Chinese had been in Limehouse in London for almost as long. There were perhaps 75,000 black and Asian people living in the whole of Britain when the *Empire Windrush*, the first immigrant ship, docked at Tilbury in June 1948.

She was an ex-German liner, converted into a British troopship, and now had some 500 West Indians on board. Some were returning to Britain having served with British forces in the war; others had come for the first time in response to a call for workers. Advertisements in the *Daily Gleaner* in Jamaica offered passage to the UK for £28 10 shillings. When they arrived, some found work immediately, most with London Transport and the NHS. Those who did not were housed in a disused deep shelter at Clapham South, last used for German and Italian PoWs. The nearest labour exchange was at Coldharbour Lane in Brixton, so this was the start of Brixton's multi-ethnic make-up.

Then, as now, there were mixed opinions about immigration. Labour backbenchers wrote to the Prime Minister complaining that a coloured influx 'is

likely to impair the harmony, strength and cohesion of our public and social life'. There was even talk in Cabinet of moving them on to Kenya. In the event, they were given a first meal of roast beef, potatoes, vegetables and Yorkshire pudding, followed by suet pudding with currants and custard – and they stayed.

The labour shortage at the start of the 1950s ensured that more immigrants followed: a Royal Commission reported that 140,000 a year were needed and employers actively recruited them. London Transport agreed with Barbados to loan the passage money for several thousand men and women from the island, to be repaid from their wages once they had arrived. Other deals were struck in Trinidad and Jamaica. British hotel and restaurant employers also began recruiting from Barbados. The biggest block of sponsored workers in the 1950s were 4500 Barbadians who were brought in by London Transport and British Railways.

Asians began arriving in numbers a bit later than West Indians. A community of Sylhettis from Bengal had lived in Spitalfields in London since before the war. They were ships' cooks who stayed on to work in Indian restaurants. Southall had concentrations of Sikhs, brought in to work in a rubber factory. Nine in ten of South Asian immigrants came from three regions: Gujarat and Punjab in India, Mirpur in Pakistan, and Sylhet in Bengal. Most were from poor rural backgrounds. They were absorbed into the iron foundries, rolling mills and furnaces of the West Midlands and Sheffield. The mills were still thriving in Lancashire and Yorkshire, and Indians and Pakistanis worked the night shifts. Some 50,000 Chinese arrived, too, from Singapore and Malaya as well as from Hong Kong and mainland China. Cypriots came as tensions flared between Turks and Greeks on their island, settling side by side in pockets in Holloway and Harringay in London. Maltese came, too.

continued on page 80

NO HOME FROM HOME
Britain had been exporting its own people around the world for the better part of 350 years. It was not so used to the arrival of others, although the great port cities, particularly London, Cardiff and Liverpool, had long had small communities of Chinese, Indians and West Indians. The first major inflows in the early 1950s were from Barbados, Trinidad and, like this girl just arrived in Southampton (left), Jamaica. They were recruited to work on the London buses, London Underground and British Rail, and soon as hospital workers. They did not always find a warm welcome. Landladies often refused to let rooms to them: 'No coloured men' says the sign (above right). In the streets – here in Brixton, South London (right) – they were often greeted with the graffiti 'KBW', short for 'Keep Britain White'.

TRANSPORT

The British were a restless people. They had explored the nooks and crannies of the globe, and had settled in many of them. Steam, in ships and railway locomotives, was in their blood. They had taken to the air, too, where they had not so long ago won one of the most critical battles in their history, the Battle of Britain.

SHIP OF EMPIRE
SS *Uganda*, a passenger-cargo liner ready for launch on the Clyde in 1952. With her sister ship, the SS *Kenya*, she plied a route from Britain to East Africa via the Suez Canal, making four trips a year.

LAST DAYS OF STEAM
The Golden Arrow, one of the two most celebrated train services in the country, is seen here in 1952 (below) with one of the last and finest of steam locomotives, the Britannia class William Shakespeare. The train pulled luxury Pullman carriages on the London Victoria to Dover route, linking up with a ferry that carried passengers to the equivalent French service from Calais to Paris. A new set of carriages was built for the train as part of the Festival of Britain. The service survived until 1972.

BIRTH OF THE JET SET

The de Havilland Comet was the world's first commercial jet airliner. It was designed by Ronald Bishop, whose design genius had produced the wartime Mosquito fighter-bomber. The Comet's smooth aerodynamics made it a machine of great beauty. Its wing was of such classic shape that it has remained in continuous civil and military use ever since. But the plane had a hidden fatal flaw.

It first flew in 1949. The test pilot was John 'Cat's Eyes' Cunningham, a famous wartime night fighter pilot: a generation of schoolboys ate up their carrots because their parents told them that was how Cunningham had acquired his legendary night vision. The Short Brothers factory in Belfast (left) was a production centre.

BOAC's first aircraft was welcomed with cheers from cabin staff as it rolled onto the tarmac at Heathrow (above) in 1952. Its first commercial service was from London to Johannesburg. Passengers were pampered in flight (below) by an 'air hostess', identified demurely as 'Miss Courtney'.

Tragedy came closer with every hour that the first Comets spent in the air. The aircraft suffered from catastrophic metal fatigue. This was deduced from painstaking examination of the wreckage after two Comets crashed in a short space of time in 1954, one off Elba and the other near Naples. The aircraft was successfully redesigned – the Nimrod version is still flying with the RAF. But Boeing's 707 caught the new market in passenger planes while the Comet was grounded.

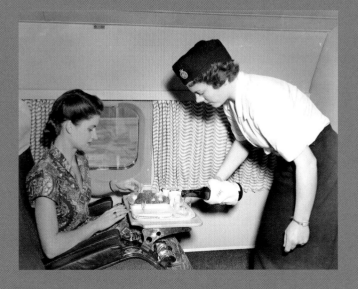

GOING TOPLESS

Britain's motor industry was booming in the 1950s. The number of cars on the road more than doubled over the decade. By 1960, some 28 per cent of households had one. Not just any old car, either. The makers of even a relatively modest family saloon, the Hillman Minx, found it worthwhile to produce a convertible model (below), as well as the 'Minx Californian' which had a bench front seat and extended roof, and there was also a Minx Estate. They were available in the 'Gay Look', which in 1950s parlance meant a two-tone colour scheme. The convertible cost £848 12 shillings when it came out in 1956, with £283 12 shillings of that going to the government in purchase tax.

The MGA (right) in 1955 was the latest in a distinguished line of MG sports cars. In those pre-breathalyser days, there were no qualms about posing for the press in front of a pub.

The production line in Vauxhall's car plant at Luton (bottom) was going full blast in 1959. But by then some of the smaller car makers were going to the wall. Alvis produced its last car, a three litre convertible, in 1955. British cars often looked good and handled well, but reliability and productivity were long-term problems.

THE NOT SO OPEN ROAD

The first parking tickets were handed out in 1958, here (below) in London's Mayfair. The absence of white lines in this picture might give the car owner reason to complain, though his distinctive number plate would be worth enough to pay many fines in today's world of vanity licence plates. Wardens were not yet pressured to issue tickets – the tax farming of road fines had not arrived – and drivers might be lucky enough to get off with a caution. But the writing was on the wall. In 1955, there were 3.6 million cars on the road. Within a decade, that would hit 9 million, and parking meters were on the way to becoming a part of the urban landscape.

It was easy to hop on a bus, though. Double-deckers had been a familiar part of the London scene since 1925. The Routemaster (left), which was introduced in 1956 to replace London's trolleybuses, was something special. Drivers loved it. The bus engineer Albert Durrant fitted it with all mod cons – power steering, an automatic gearbox and hydraulic brakes. Passengers were enamoured, too, by the details used by designer Douglas Scott, like its wind-down windows and 'lovers' seat' at the back. And the open back allowed people to hop on and off wherever it was most convenient. The Routemaster gave sterling service for half a century.

The economy and housing

The economic recovery was jerky, and was already developing the boom-or-bust disease that would stay with it for many years to come, but it continued. Housing was a particular success. Harold Macmillan, the housing minister, managed to meet his much publicised target of 300,000 homes a year. New homes were mainly flats, though still on a human scale, being low-rise with five storeys or less.

The first crop of new towns that had been started after the war – Stevenage, Harlow, Crawley, Bracknell, Basildon, Corby, Peterlee, Aycliffe and the like – grew rapidly. Three bedroom semi-detacheds on new estates in the South started from around £1500, at a time when a skilled worker could expect to make a little over £1000 a year. At Crawley New Town, the construction company Taylor Woodrow was advertising the 'House of Tomorrow', with fitted kitchen and Formica tops, for £2195. It was open plan, for 'clutter' was frowned on. Many a Victorian and Edwardian terrace house was about to have its picture rail, dadoes, skirting boards and ornate fireplaces stripped out in the name of modernisation.

The car industry was booming. The Ford Popular was launched in 1953 as the cheapest car on the market. It bought the open road within reach of practically everyone: in 1954 it cost £390 (of which £115 was purchase tax). It had no heater, no glove compartment, no sun visor or warning lights, no ashtray, radio or map pockets, but who cared? What it did come with was a starting handle and a choice of black, blue or grey. *Motor* magazine reported that it 'is more than able to keep up with other traffic, accelerating briskly even without skilled use of the gearbox'. In contrast, the big Ford Zodiac, introduced in 1954, was capable of doing 100mph, and came with two-speed wipers, loop pile carpets, arm rests, ash trays and a cigar lighter.

For sheer flamboyance, though, the public had to wait for the Golden Zebra Daimler Coupe in 1955. It was built especially for Lady Norah Docker, the wondrously flamboyant wife of long-suffering Sir Bernard, chairman of Daimler. It cost £12,000 in 1955 – enough to buy 30 Ford Populars and still come away with change. It had an ivory dashboard, gold plating inside and out, and zebra-hide upholstery, hence its name. Asked why she chose zebra, Lady Docker replied: 'Because mink is too hot to sit on.' She took the car to the wedding of Hollywood actress Grace Kelly and Prince Rainier in Monte Carlo – it was rarely 'Monaco' then – where she burnt a Monegasque flag and was expelled, by official account, or left in disgust, by her own. Lady Docker brought some much-needed bling to the Fifties, and was applauded and disapproved of in equal measure.

BREAKING THE MOULD

To the headline writers, the great achievers of 1954 were Roger Bannister and Lester Piggott. On 6 May, 1954, Bannister ran the mile in 3 minutes 59.4 seconds, becoming the first man in the world to run the mile in under 4 minutes. Piggott was the youngest ever Derby winner, aged just 18, on Never Say Die.

The British had invented or adapted most of the world's favourite sports. They were 'not outstandingly good at them', noted George Orwell, the great

essayist and novelist, who died at only 47 in 1950. 'But they enjoy playing them and to an extent that strikes foreigners as childish, they enjoy reading about them and betting on them.'

The changing face of entertainment

Another old amusement, music hall, that mixture of bawdiness, patriotism and fun, was in serious decline. Hippodromes and Alhambras were reduced to bingo or even the wreckers' ball. They held on in the big resorts and still had some stars: Gracie Fields, George Formby and Max Miller, the 'Cheeky Chappie' in kipper tie, florid plus-fours, white trilby and diamond rings. Miller used to ask his audience if they wanted clean jokes from his white gag book, and always looked puzzled when they opted for the blue.

The Christmas Panto was still a much-loved ritual. Radio, TV and film comedies kept the old artistry alive. *Saturday Night at the London Palladium* was a television celebration of the whole genre. The BBC signed up a series in 1953 with Morecambe and Wise, two of the most brilliant performers. It was called *Running Wild*, and was a monster flop. One press review read, 'Definition of the

BREAKING THE MILE BARRIER
In 1954, Roger Bannister (centre) ran the mile in 3 minutes 59.4 seconds at the Iffley Road track in Oxford, becoming the first man to break through the 4-minute barrier. He was paced by two other famous names in athletics, Christopher Chataway (right) and Chris Brasher (left). Bannister's achievement continued the country's fine tradition of medium-distance running. All three men were amateurs: Highland Games apart, few athletes ran for money then. Later that year Bannister retired from athletics competition to concentrate on medicine and went on to have a distinguished career as a neurologist.

'I can't see it [rock-and-roll] ever becoming a real craze.'

Ted Heath, bandleader

Week: TV set – the box in which they buried Morecambe and Wise.' They recovered, though, with successful spots on *The Winifred Atwell Show*, and would eventually go on to become huge TV stars.

The music world was about to have its biggest shake-up in years as rock-and-roll arrived from America. In 1954 Bill Haley and his Comets recorded the seminal rock-and-roll anthem, *Rock Around the Clock*. The song shot Haley to stardom the following year after it was heard on the soundtrack of *Blackboard Jungle*, an MGM film about juvenile delinquency starring Sidney Poitier and Glenn Ford. But even before then the record was a hit in Britain: in January 1955, months before it charted in the US, it reached Number 17 in the chart of the *New Musical Express*, itself less than three years old. John Lennon recalled it as his first rock-and-roll experience. The next year Elvis Presley's *Blue Suede Shoes* climbed the charts and pop music never looked back, although not everyone recognised it at the time. Bandleader Ted Heath insisted that rock-and-roll had no future in Britain. 'It is primarily for coloured people,' he said, 'I can't see it ever becoming a real craze.' TV critic John Crosby, meanwhile, dismissed Elvis as an 'unspeakable, untalented and vulgar young entertainer'. How wrong could they be?

Winnie bows out

Churchill resigned in April 1955 and was succeeded by Anthony Eden. The new Prime Minister was all charm and ability on the surface, but shyness, loneliness and nerves were not far below. 'Part mad baronet, part beautiful woman', his Tory rival R A Butler cruelly said of him.

Eden was born into a landed family in County Durham. A highly strung child, he had a classic Eton and Oxford education. He fought on the Somme in the First World War, winning an MC in 1917, and was lucky to survive. Two of his brothers were killed in the trenches, and his much-loved son Simon was killed in an air crash in Burma in 1945.

THE ROCK-AND-ROLL REVOLUTION
The queues went round the block when the film *Rock Around the Clock*, featuring Bill Haley and His Comets, opened across the country. This one is waiting to get into the Gaiety Cinema in Manchester in 1956. Haley was an ex-country and western singer, with a spit curl and a band in matching plaid jackets. Before long he would be eclipsed by the younger, more handsome and more talented Elvis Presley, while local boys with manufactured names such as Vince Eager and Tommy Quickly also joined the rock-and-roll action. But Haley's *Rock Around the Clock* single sold 25 million copies worldwide, and he was, if briefly, the first face of Rock in Britain.

Eden's political career was dazzling. He became foreign secretary in 1935, while still in his thirties. Three years later he resigned over the appeasement of Mussolini, the Italian fascist leader who had invaded Ethiopia. He was close to Churchill, the great anti-appeaser, and married his niece Clarissa. Eden returned to government as foreign minister with Churchill in 1940, a skilful, charming and immensely hard-working man. Back in the wilderness with Churchill in 1945, he was a much-respected shadow minister before returning to the front bench in 1951. Though he seldom showed it, he had endured a frustrating ten years as heir apparent, as the old man hung on and on.

Eden's premiership started on a wave of good feeling. He was well-liked for his modesty and trusted for his vast experience.

Eden called an election immediately he became Prime Minister, and won it handsomely. His majority was 60, where Churchill had only a 16-seat surplus in 1951, and Attlee had limped through in 1950 with just 5. So Eden's premiership started on a wave of good feeling. He was well-liked for his modesty and trusted for his vast experience. But he was not a fit man. He overworked, suffered appendicitis and jaundice, and was prey to migraines and gallstones. A slip of the surgeon's knife which accidentally cut his biliary duct during a simple gall bladder operation in 1953 had caused lasting damage. He lost large quantities of blood, his recovery was slow and his resilience much undermined. His parliamentary public secretary, Robert Carr, said that afterwards he was 'never the same man'.

The usual government problems – the economy, balance of payments worries, strikes – were made worse by tensions within Eden's Cabinet. Its two leading members, Butler and Harold Macmillan, were both ambitious for Eden's job. Before long, it was whispered that he was a sick man, that he was weak and indecisive, and that he should go. *The Daily Telegraph* carried a stinging piece at the beginning of 1956. Headed 'The Firm Smack of Government', it went on to say that Eden did not have it and that he was capable only of 'smoothing and fixing'. By-election defeats in the Spring soured the mood more, but for Eden things were about to get a whole lot worse.

WINNIE'S FAREWELL
Hallmark cigar glowing, Churchill bids Anthony Eden good luck as he hands over to him as Prime Minister in 1955. Eden, who had been foreign secretary as early as 1935, had lived and worked in the great man's shadow since 1940. He had waited patiently, but when his time came, his health was no longer robust. Though he began as a popular successor to Churchill, events were to show that he was already past his prime.

THE SUEZ CRISIS AND BIRTH OF CONSUMERISM

In Egypt, a dynamic young colonel called Gamal Abdul Nasser was making potent anti-British speeches. They were the first stirrings of the Suez Crisis, an event that would bring down the Prime Minister, Anthony Eden, and prove a watershed in British history.

TEENAGE KICKS The records were still 78s, but the rock-and-roll music was brand new.

EDEN AND SUEZ

Nasser, the son of a postal clerk, had risen through the ranks of the Egyptian army and come to power two years after King Farouk had gone into luxurious exile in Italy following a coup by nationalist army officers. He wanted the British out of their bases in the Canal Zone, a strip of land running for 120 miles alongside the Suez Canal, with its airfields, depots, parade grounds and barracks, and 40,000 British troops. The British agreed to go, but Nasser kept tweaking the imperial tail, refusing to join the British-backed Baghdad Pact for regional security and flirting with the Soviets.

In March 1956, King Hussein of Jordan sacked Sir John Glubb, 'Glubb Pasha' to the British press, something of a second Lawrence of Arabia and the British commander of Jordan's Arab Legion. The sacking was a humiliation to Britain, confirming Nasser's influence. It provoked the normally suave prime minister into telephoning Anthony Nutting, the Foreign Office minister, and having him dragged from a diplomatic dinner at the Savoy. He told Nutting that it was 'poppycock' for the Foreign Office to talk of 'isolating' Nasser. 'I want him destroyed, can't you understand?' he bellowed. 'I don't give a damn if there's anarchy and chaos in Egypt.' From here on, Nutting recalled, Eden lost his touch. 'Gone was his old uncanny sense of timing, his deft feel for negotiations.' Driven by pride and prestige, and nagged by sickness, he began to behave 'like an enraged elephant'.

Raising the stakes

In July, the British and Americans announced that they would no longer provide $200 million previously pledged to build the Aswan High Dam. This was Nasser's pet project, and he took it as a personal insult. He made his response to a huge crowd in Alexandria on the anniversary of the overthrow of the monarchy. He spoke of Egyptians being kept waiting by British High Commissioners and ambassadors in the past. Now things would change. 'Today', he said, 'in the same way that Farouk left us on July 26, the old Suez Canal also leaves us on the same day.' Eden was dining with the Iraqi prime minister in London when a message was handed to him: 'Nasser has nationalised the Suez Canal.'

Early opinion at home was bellicose. 'Grabber Nasser', said the *Daily Mirror*, while *The Times* dropped its normal courtesy of acknowledging his rank of colonel, and referred simply to 'Nasser'. The Americans were more low-key. President Eisenhower was to run for re-election in the autumn, and he was in no mood for Middle East adventures. Eden broadcast to the nation on 8 August. He said the quarrel was not with Egypt, 'still less the Arab world', but with Nasser himself. He reminded people of 'what the cost can be of giving in to fascism', an appeal to the past, and in particular his own past. As time drifted, however, so did support for an invasion. 'Grand Old Anthony Eden', they said, marching his men to the top of the hill and marching them down again. He was sleeping badly, his diary shows. His wife was unwell.

A NATION DIVIDED
The crowds who gathered in Trafalgar Square in early November 1956 knew that Israeli troops had moved into Egypt on 29 October, that RAF bombers had left their bases in Cyprus to attack targets in Egypt on 31 October, and that a British invasion force was at sea in the Mediterranean. What they did not know was that French envoys had been at Chequers on 14 October to propose a secret Anglo-French-Israeli attack to topple Nasser, or that clandestine talks had opened near Paris on 22 October. A secret protocol was agreed in which Israel would attack Egypt, then Britain and France would invade as 'peacemakers' to separate the warring sides. But the protestors demanding 'Law not War' suspected that something was afoot. The most divisive issue for a generation, Suez split public opinion down the middle.

THE ADVERSARIES
Anthony Eden meets his nemesis, Egypt's President Gamal Nasser, in Cairo in 1955. A year later, Nasser nationalised the Suez Canal. Eden took it as an almost personal insult. His wife Clarissa said she felt as if 'the Suez Canal was flowing through the drawing room' at 10 Downing Street. For his part, Nasser was outraged that Britain and America had withdrawn a pledge to finance the Aswan High Dam because of his links with the Soviets.

But Eden was not the only one with a score to settle with Nasser. The French and Israelis held secret meetings in Paris at the end of September. Quite apart from the Suez Canal, the French were angered by his support for the Algerian nationalists they were fighting. For their part, the Israelis wanted to attack him before, as they suspected, he attacked them. The two agreed to act in concert.

A French delegation went to Chequers on 14 October. Why did the British not join them? Eden could not resist. A secret deal was put together in Sevres, a Paris suburb. Israel was to invade Egypt on the evening of 29 October and reach the canal. The British and French, feigning ignorance, would then appeal to both sides to stop fighting, withdraw ten miles from the canal, and accept a Franco-British occupation of the Zone to guarantee unhindered passage for shipping.

The plan goes into action

Israeli armour duly rattled into the Sinai. As predicted, Nasser rejected the Franco-British ultimatum. On 31 October, waves of Canberras, flying from airfields in Cyprus, began bombing Egyptian air bases. Air superiority was easily won, with 260 Egyptian aircraft destroyed for the loss of one French and two RAF pilots.

CAUSE OF THE CRISIS
The Suez Canal is 100 miles long, allowing ships to pass from Asia to Europe without going all the way round Africa. It was opened to traffic in 1869 and in 1875 the British bought the Egyptian government's holding in the canal, to become joint owners with the French. In 1881, it was declared a neutral zone under British protection. In 1954, the British agreed to leave. Nasser nationalised the canal in 1956 to raise the revenues to pay for the new Aswan High Dam. At the start of the invasion, he ordered merchant ships to be sunk to block the canal. By the time this picture was taken, on 19 November, 1956, the naval vessel on the right was already carrying out salvage operations.

Nasser had blocked the canal by sinking merchant ships passing through it, but Egypt's defences were smashed. British and French troops were not yet on the ground – the naval task force was still cruising down the Mediterranean from Malta to Port Said. In the early hours of 5 November, British and French paratroops were dropped to seize the airfields and key bridges around Port Said and Port Suez. Ground troops went in off the boats at dawn the next morning. By nightfall on 6 November, Egyptian resistance was finished. The British and French lost 32 men. The Egyptians, utterly outgunned, lost more than 2000.

Militarily, it was a triumph. Politically, it was a fiasco. The Soviets, themselves facing a popular uprising in Hungary, were threatening to support Nasser, so the Cold War was becoming uncomfortably warm. Washington had come out firmly against the venture. The next morning, gold and dollars began haemorrhaging from British reserves. The chancellor, Harold Macmillan, telephoned Washington to ask for help in the currency crisis. He was told in no uncertain terms that support would only come if a ceasefire was arranged. Before the day's cabinet meeting, Macmillan told the foreign secretary, Selwyn Lloyd, that the financial and economic pressures were so great that 'we must stop'.

MONEY TALKS

The Anglo-French invasion was a near flawless military triumph – and a copper-bottomed diplomatic and financial disaster. These British soldiers at Suez (below) pose happily on a British-made artillery piece captured from Egyptian forces after the British landing at Port Said on 6 November. But no sooner had the troops got ashore, rapidly overcoming Egyptian resistance, than they were stopped. On that same day, Eden's cabinet voted to call off the invasion and the troops were halted after advancing just 23 miles down the canal. The weakness of sterling was decisive. Washington disapproved of the venture, and made it clear that the Americans would do nothing to help London avoid financial melt-down unless it was called off.

Eden was faced by hostility from Washington and the United Nations, the unspoken threat of Russian intervention, the fears of the Treasury, and subtle but unmistakable signs from his colleagues that they had no intention of going down with a ship that was already low in the water. In the early afternoon, President Eisenhower was told that Britain would agree to a ceasefire. British tanks were clattering south to take complete control of the canal, moving at speed and meeting no resistance. That night, they were ordered to halt. 'The Americans have stopped the advance', they were told.

End of the road for Eden

The Prime Minister was a broken man when he went to the Commons to announce the decision. Amid cheers and jeers, he slumped on the front bench, his face grey, save where the 'black rimmed caverns surrounded the dying embers of his eyes'. His 'whole personality seemed completely withdrawn', for this was a personal calamity, a prime minister utterly undone in the field of foreign affairs, to which he had devoted most of his life, a humiliation unequalled in the century.

It was one that Washington was at pains to rub in. Had some British troops remained in Egypt as part of the United Nations peacekeeping forces, at least a fig leaf of respectability for the Suez adventure would have remained. The Americans vetoed it. Sterling was not to be propped up until all British forces left Port Said unconditionally. It seemed scant recompense for British loyalty in containing communism in Berlin, Korea and Malaya. But Eden's colleagues, Macmillan prominent among them, were just as eager to undermine him.

Eden was exhausted. His doctors advised a total change of scenery, so on 23 November he flew with his wife to Jamaica to stay at Goldeneye, the hideaway of Ian Fleming, creator of James Bond and a personal friend. Three weeks later he was back, rested but warned that his health was too undermined for him to continue at Number Ten. In the early evening of 9 January, 1957, he drove to Buckingham Palace to tender his resignation to the Queen. Within a fortnight he was gone, on a cruise to New Zealand. His cabin steward was John Prescott, a man almost his exact opposite in terms of elegance of dress, speech and manner, but more than his equal, perhaps, in toughness of character. They got on famously. Eden returned to a quite retirement and died in 1977, aged 79.

A NEW BROOM

Macmillan took over. Butler's hostility to the Suez invasion ruled him out as party leader as far as the Tory backwoodsmen were concerned. Macmillan had opposed it, too, when he saw the way the wind was blowing, but he had hidden it better. He was skilled at dissimulation. His natural habitat appeared to be the grouse moor. He had the air of an Edwardian grandee, and to a degree, he was.

His background was Eton, Oxford and the Guards, and he was married to the daughter of the Duke of Devonshire, quite one of the grandest people in the country. He would have been in trouble had he relied on this – deference and the class system came more and more under fire from the young as the decade

CHANGING OF THE GUARD
The Labour giants of the 1940s were beached in the new decade. Aneurin Bevan (far right), scourge of the bourgeoisie a few years before, is mimicked by a small boy during the 1955 election campaign, which saw the Tories back with an increased majority. Bevan was replaced as a Labour star by Harold Wilson, pictured here (near right) with his trademark pipe, and Labour's rising female star, Barbara Castle. Richard Austen Butler, always known by his initials, 'RAB', was the heavyweight Tory thinker, responsible for the 1944 Education Act which had reorganised secondary education and set up the 'eleven plus'. He had been chancellor in Churchill's last cabinet. It was thought that he would succeed Eden as Prime Minister, but he lacked Macmillan's easy charm. Harold Macmillan, seen here (main picture) during a grouse shoot on the moors near Masham in Yorkshire, was a man with the common touch. He had a keen eye for the main chance as well as game birds and he knew how to massage public opinion.

POLITICAL FACES OLD AND NEW

progressed. But his grandfather had been born a Scottish crofter who had grown up to make his fortune in publishing. And as a politician, Macmillan had the common touch, a bubbling optimism and a showman's flair.

His main drive was for prosperity and social consensus. As a young MP for Stockton-on-Tees before the war, he had seen the immense damage done by mass unemployment, and this coloured his political outlook. His chancellor, Heathcoat Amory, said 'He was terrified of one thing, a slump'. He would ring Amory up and ask, 'Do you think there will be a slump next month?'

'You've never had it so good'

Macmillan's famous phrase came from a speech that he made at Bedford football ground in 1957. 'Let's be frank about it,' he said, 'most of our people have never had it so good.' To go round the country, to visit individual towns and farms, was to see a prosperity not seen 'in my lifetime, nor indeed ever in the history of this country'.

What is less well-remembered is that he went on to qualify his statement. 'Is this too good to last?', he worried. Would rising prices be the beast that killed off this prosperity? Was it possible to maintain steady prices, full employment and an expanding economy? 'Can we control inflation?' he asked. 'This is the problem of our time.' It was indeed. The cycle of boom-bust-boom had arrived.

The headline writers ignored the caution, of course, and in any case, the first part was true – people were better off than ever before. Average earnings in the five years to 1960 rose 37 per cent. At the same time, the price of televisions, gramophones, refrigerators, washing machines, vacuum cleaners and other mass-produced products was falling in real terms. Televisions and electric irons were the most popular domestic items, with four in five households owning both by the end of the decade. Vacuum cleaners came next, followed by washing machines – not yet automatic ones – with fridges trailing behind; only one family in four had a fridge in the kitchen.

Car ownership was the most visible change. It rocketed by 250 per cent over the decade. The arrival of parking tickets in 1958 was one symptom, though wardens were not yet on bonus incentives, and three tickets was a day's work for some. Ferocious rush hours were another result, particularly in London, where the number of private cars topped the one million mark.

The young in particular had money to spend and the Teddy Boys spent some of theirs on dressing in style. Their name came from their Edwardian-style draped jackets with velvet collars, which they wore with drainpipe trousers and thick-soled shoes. Lashings of hair cream were used to sculpt Tony Curtis-style quiffs. Elsewhere, it was not a vintage decade for fashion. Wigs – jet black, red,

continued on page 102

SHOESHINE
New models for him and her were brought out by K shoes (left) to celebrate the Festival of Britain. Like other manufacturers at the time, they were a family firm dating back to Robert Miller, who first started making shoes in Kendal in 1842. They later merged with Clarks, who pipped them to the post. Their first sheepskin slippers dated from 1830.

'YOUR M&S'
A floor level view of customers at one of the
company's 234 stores in 1955. It was 'Marks
and Sparks' to most people and it benefited
hugely from the long boom that saw average
wages almost double over the decade. Its
profits quadrupled in the 10 years from 1948.
Sir Simon Marks spent heavily on market
research to predict new trends before his
competitors. M&S was so sure of customer
loyalty, though, that it thought it unnecessary
to advertise when ITV was launched, a
mistake that later cost it dear.

BRAVE NEW WORLD OF SHOPPING

In a way, the 1950s were a continuation of the 1930s, when affluence had started working its way down the social order in earnest – at least in the booming Southeast and Midlands. This time, although these areas again did best, it was a more general phenomenon, because employment had recovered in the textiles and heavy industries in the North and Scotland.

SHOPPING HEAVEN
'White goods' like these (above) did away with much drudgery. The wash-day toil for housewives was in large part alleviated by clothes washers. Refrigerators kept food fresh, so it was no longer necessary to shop every day for food. Electric ovens and hobs were a vast improvement on cooking on coal or coke in the many places not connected to mains gas. Dish-washing machines were still beyond most pockets, but they were at least on the horizon. A woman irons in the corner of a kitchen (left) that is well-equipped by the standards of only a few years before, with a gas geyser for instant hot water.

The Incre...

98

THE BOX

Television came of age in the 1950s. By the end of the decade, there were 10 million sets in use across the country. Children were such eager viewers that a 'Toddler's Truce' was enforced between 6pm and 7pm, when programmes were shut down to allow mums to get children to bed without tantrums at being torn away from the TV. ITV lobbied hard to end the practice, as it cost them money from lost commercials.

SMALL CAR, BIG HEART

The Morris Mini was a truly revolutionary car when it was introduced in 1959. It was designed by Alec Issigonis, who had fashioned the equally loved Morris Minor. His chief innovation was to use a transverse front-wheel drive engine – that is, he turned the engine around 90 degrees to create more space inside the car – and this meant that a quart could be crammed into the Mini's pint pot. Whether it could have managed this load down to the last poodle on the road, as opposed to a 1959 publicity studio shot, is open to doubt. But it was an incredible car – and it came as an Austin Seven for those who liked it better that way.

AUSTIN SEVEN &
MORRIS MINI-MINOR

HELP YOURSELF

The big high-street innovations were supermarkets and self-service stores, like this one in Westbourne Grove in London in 1950. The first supermarket was generally reckoned to be a branch of Sainsbury's in Croydon that advertised 'Q-less' shopping. Instead of queuing at individual counters, there was now just a check-out queue, though that could stretch back, too. The big grocery chains loved them, because they employed fewer people. 'Staff-less' they were, shelf-stackers and check-out girls apart, and with a vengeance. In 1947, there were only 10 self-service stores in the whole country. By 1956, there were 3000, and that figure quadrupled over the next six years. They were impersonal places, with none of the friendly banter and sense of community that permeated the corner shops and grocers they replaced. They were bland and had less sense of place. But they stocked a huge range of goods, they were clean, bright and efficient, and they were cheaper. Shoplifting increased, however. Unlike shops with the physical barrier of a counter, open-plan stores and supermarkets were an invitation to the light-fingered.

STOCKING UP
In pre-refrigerator days, food did not keep for long in the larder, the part of the kitchen where food was stored on marble shelves, with wire-mesh fly screens to protect meat, fish and cheese. Many housewives popped out to the shops once or even twice a day, to the baker, the butcher, the fishmonger, the greengrocer. Retailers could now stock a wider range of food, much of it protected by sheets of Perspex left over from making aircraft canopies during the war. Perishable items could be stored in refrigerated cabinets. So the weekly shop, a boon for working mothers, became more common.

LA CRÈME DE LA CRÈME
The well-heeled in London bought their luxury goods in Piccadilly. Here, the doorman hails a taxi for ladies leaving Fortnum and Mason, the luxury food store that dates back to 1707. Close links with the East India Company meant that Fortnums always dealt with the most exotic, not to say most expensive, foods from around the world. The British had a historic love of curry and other Indian spices and foods. In the 1950s, they began slowly adventuring in food again, with Mediterranean ingredients becoming much favoured.

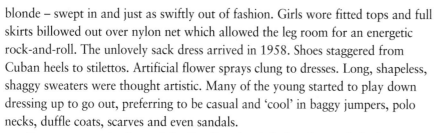

blonde – swept in and just as swiftly out of fashion. Girls wore fitted tops and full skirts billowed out over nylon net which allowed the leg room for an energetic rock-and-roll. The unlovely sack dress arrived in 1958. Shoes staggered from Cuban heels to stilettos. Artificial flower sprays clung to dresses. Long, shapeless, shaggy sweaters were thought artistic. Many of the young started to play down dressing up to go out, preferring to be casual and 'cool' in baggy jumpers, polo necks, duffle coats, scarves and even sandals.

Jeans were coming in, and the first 'boutique' clothes shop to help the young spend their new-found wealth opened in the King's Road, Chelsea, in 1955. It was called Bazaar and was started by two former art students, Mary Quant and Alexander Plunkett. Here were the first stirrings of the clothes and retail revolution that was to produce the Carnaby Street phenomenon a decade later.

Rise of the 'never never'

The credit society was just beginning. The ending of hire purchase restrictions in 1958 gave a big boost to the sale of cars, furniture and kitchen appliances. Commonly known as the 'never never', hire purchase led to a big rise in personal debt. Churchmen and others complained about the burgeoning consumer society. Archbishop Fisher criticised the 'temptations to self-indulgence', which he said accounted for 'a great deal of the world's sin and misery'. The perils of easy

STYLE FOR GIRLS …
An avant garde young woman, in 1953 a pioneer of blue jeans, window shops in London (above). Blue jeans were just beginning to become popular among the young, heavily influenced by charismatic film stars like Marlon Brando and James Dean, who wore them in hit films. By 1957, 150 million pairs were being sold worldwide. These two young women (left), on holiday in Blackpool, stayed faithful to a more traditionally feminine look, one even wearing gloves, though the desire for elegance is not helped by eating candy floss on the street. The famous comedian Arthur Askey was topping the bill in the theatre they are walking past.

... AND STYLE FOR BOYS

Smart grooming was the order of the day in the 1950s – even teenage Teddy boys, the troublemakers of the era, were immaculately coiffed and suited. The name 'Teddy boys' was coined by the Daily Express in 1953. They wore long draped jackets, often as here with velvet trim collar and pocket flaps, waistcoats, and 'slim jim' ties and 'Mr B' shirt collars, as worn by the jazzman Billy Eckstine. These outfits were tailor-made and did not come cheap. Contrary to their public image, most 'Teds' worked hard in well-paid jobs, even if their weekend behaviour was not always perfect.

NOT A HAIR OUT OF PLACE

Liberal amounts of Brylcreem were used to mould men's hair into shape. For Teds, as the decade progressed, this meant an increasingly pronounced quiff over the forehead. And not to worry if it started to droop during an evening out – the ubiquitous men's hair unction could be bought by the dab from vending machines.

BRYLCREEM

grooms by surface tension

LET YOUR SCALP

END OF A KILLER

The first polio vaccine, developed by Jonas Salk, was announced in 1955. It consisted of an injected dose of killed poliovirus. These children are waiting with their mothers for their jabs outside a Middlesex County Council Clinic in 1956, at the beginning of the campaign to vaccinate every child in the county. Before the introduction of vaccinations, polio was a terrible scourge. Treatment involved months lying in an 'iron lung', which did the breathing for victims while paralysed by the disease. Those lucky enough to survive were often crippled. Pioneers like Salk, or Fleming with penicillin, were well known and much admired in a society that still knew what it was to live through lethal epidemics.

credit were seen in the film *Live Now, Pay Later*, which showed a salesman foisting furniture on housewives who didn't need it.

Macmillan himself would have none of what he called these 'superior people' who denounced HP as encouraging the 'feckless' among the working class. 'The temptations of comfort and affluence are not an argument in favour of poverty', he insisted. He was not ashamed of his 'having it so good' speech – 'our purpose should be to keep it good and make it better'. He said that he was happy to get stuck in traffic at weekends when he drove to Birch Grove, his country house in Sussex, because the other cars were filled with families going to the seaside. The same people ten years before 'would have spent the weekend in back streets'.

High-rise housing policy

The outpouring of consumer goods was increasingly installed in new high-rise blocks of flats. The trend began under Duncan Sandys, who had taken Macmillan's old job as housing minister during Eden's government. Prior to 1955, all public sector housing attracted the same grant. Sandys changed this by

continued on page 109

INNOVATIONS IN HEALTH CARE

Early diagnosis was one weapon against diseases such as tuberculosis (TB); another was penicillin, the new wonder-drug discovered in the previous decade. Streptomycin was making TB far less lethal than it had been, but it was still a serious problem: in 1955 there were 50,000 new cases of the disease.

Radiography equipment was one of the main tools of diagnosis. Mobile units aimed to offer X-rays to as many people as possible across the country. This picture, taken on 11 March, 1957, was part of a publicity campaign staged by Glasgow's Health Department to raise awareness of the disease and to increase attendance at the X-ray sessions.

THE CHANGING FACE OF HOUSING

A PLACE TO LIVE

Many industrial Victorian terraces remained, with their back yards housing the outside toilet and separated by a back lane. These (left) are in Newcastle in 1950: row upon row of such streets led down towards the Tyne. But new towns, airy, grassy, healthy, were being built to replace them at a rapid pace, at Aycliffe, Bracknell, Corby, Crawley, Harlow, Peterlee, Stevenage and here (above), Hemel Hempstead in Hertfordshire. They lacked much of the neighbourliness and soul of the urban terrace streets, as well as the corner pubs and shops, the buses and bustle. Townies were not used to countryside, but they had their own front doors, and plenty of greenery and trees, and the children soon adapted. High-rise blocks like these (below) on the Brandon Estate, Southwark, then London's highest, could easily degenerate into vertical slums. The pre-fabs at their feet were built rapidly to alleviate the housing shortage after the war. The trend to build upwards accelerated after 1955, when council high-rise was given larger subsidies than houses.

allocating more to high-rise homes, on the grounds that per square foot they cost less to build than medium-rise and thus were more efficient.

The people who were decanted into these soulless towers never liked them, and soon yearned for their familiar terraces and back-to-backs, however down-at-heel. A council house, with a garden, fitted kitchen, proper bathroom and central heating, was a marvel to those from the slums. But in a high-rise flat parents worried about their children and how they could keep an eye on them from a hundred feet up in the sky. They missed the sense of neighbourliness, and the focus on the street with its gossip and street parties on high days. A terrace house was a family bastion, with its own front door, where the tower blocks were compared to giant battery chicken coops. But politicians and planners loved them, and the proportion of high-rise in public housing leapt from 3 to 15 per cent by 1960, on its way to reaching 26 per cent by the mid-1960s.

At the same time, more people were buying their own homes. The proportion of owner occupiers rose from 31 to 44 per cent over the decade. Those renting from landlords fell from just over half to 31 per cent, with an increase in council properties and New Town housing taking up the rest.

THE PITS
Coalmining and the pit villages had their own distinctive culture. They were shot through with celebrated colliery brass bands, male voice choirs, pigeon and whippet racing, banners, parades, with playing cricket in County Durham and Yorkshire, rugby in Wales, with the growing of giant leeks, with chapel-going and the Labour Party. Politicians were frightened of men like these tough Welsh colliers (left) who have just come off shift. Harold Macmillan said that no sane man would ever take on the Roman Catholic Church, the Brigade of Guards or the National Union of Mineworkers. He never did while he was Prime Minister – when Edward Heath eventually did so, the NUM destroyed him – and the result was that miners' pay and conditions vastly improved over the decade.

The recruiting poster (above) was correct in saying that lads learnt a trade in the pits. Britain's deep mines needed skills in many fields – engineering and electrical work of all sorts, construction, explosives, transport, geology, surveying and more. Life might be brutish in a pit, but the men who manned it were far from brutes.

A CHANGING SOCIETY

Social mobility was greatly on the increase. By the mid-1950s, only one man in three had the same social status as his father. Only one in four of labourers' sons remained unskilled. But Macmillan's fears of economic backsliding were real. With near full employment, there was less inhibition about striking for higher pay and thus stoking inflation. A national newspaper strike in 1955 lasted for four weeks, a rail strike a fortnight, and a London bus strike three years later went on for seven weeks. Demarcation disputes between unions were increasing, and so were unofficial 'wildcat' strikes.

Labour relations were caught to comic perfection in the film *I'm All Right, Jack*, starring Peter Sellers as the pompous Marxist shop steward Kite. Terry-Thomas played the hapless factory manager, who says of the strikers besieging his office: 'They are the kind of chaps who don't wear pyjamas when they're in bed.' A sourness often hung between workers and bosses, and even between workers and workers. More disturbingly another film, *The Angry Silence*, showed the violent fate of a blackleg who refused to join an unofficial strike.

Macmillan timed his boom well as the decade built towards a personal high note. The tabloids dubbed him 'Supermac' after a cartoon that sniped at him as a make-believe Superman was stripped of its irony and used as affectionate praise. He won the 1959 election with a 100-seat majority. A Trog cartoon showed him in an armchair chatting to a car, a full fridge, washing machine and television. 'Well, gentlemen', he says, 'I think we all fought a good fight ...'

EARNING A CRUST

Ever productive, these Wellington-booted fishwives at Great Yarmouth (left) are knitting while they wait for the boats to come in during the East Anglian herring season. Their job was to gut, sort and pack the fish. The herring might then be smoked to produce fine kippers, a much-loved breakfast delicacy across the land.

Another taste, the nation's sweet tooth, was catered for by some of the 4300 women employed by Cadbury's (below right) at its Bournville factory. With sweets and chocolate off ration, production was going flat out. Everyone liked a flutter, too, on the Derby, the Grand National and the weekly football pools. Millions of football pool coupons were dealt with every week by the women (below left) in the offices of this Liverpool pools firm in 1954.

WOMEN'S WORK

There was more to it than that, of course. After long years of effort and striving, the British had begun to enjoy themselves and Supermac reaped the political reward. The country as a whole was relatively problem free.

Scots nationalists had started the decade by hijacking the Stone of Scone, the ancient inaugural stone of the Scottish kings, from Westminster Abbey. It was returned, though, and the Scottish Nationalist Party enjoyed little electoral support. With the demand for post-war rebuilding, jobs and good wages were reliably on offer in the shipyards, heavy engineering, steel mills and mines of Lanark, Ayrshire, Glasgow and the Clyde. These traditional industries were all teetering towards a precipice, with swelling competition from the Far East, but they had not reached it yet.

The same held true of the shipyards and textile mills of Northern Ireland. Average incomes had been a scant 55 per cent of UK levels just before the war, but the boom since had seen them rise to 68 per cent. New housing had gone up

WORKING TO THE FACTORY WHISTLE
Workers from the Camperdown Mills in Dundee stream out of the factory gate the moment the knocking-off whistle sounds. Like other traditional industries, the Dundee jute mills were about to start taking body blows from artificial fibres and from ferocious competition from Asia – and people would soon be more eager to stay in work than to leave it.

THE CITY GENT
When the railwaymen came out on strike in 1955, this City worker took to a scooter for his daily commute. Over the decades to come, the City was to prove itself adaptable to changing conditions. Briefcase neatly tucked behind him, bowler hat serving as a crash helmet (they were not yet compulsory), and driving his diminutive machine with the same air of authority as a police escort rider, he shows that nothing should ruffle the determined commuter. The same year, the government announced a £212-million road modernisation programme, including motorways, the first of which – the Preston Bypass, now part of the M6 – opened in December 1958. The first stretch of the M1 was opened the following November.

at a gallop in the province over the decade. Warning signs of a coming downturn were evident, and the fault line separating the two communities of Protestant and Catholic, loyalist and nationalist, ran through almost everything – schooling, housing, sport, employment, prospects. Resentments were simmering, but the boiling point, and sectarian violence, were still a few years off.

The second half of the decade was a period of general 'easement'. This produced its own paradox: as prosperity increased, so did crime. Since Victorian days, need and deprivation had been seen as the triggers for crime. By this theory, as both diminished after 1955, crime should also have fallen. But it didn't. It went up – particularly among the young, who had benefited most of all. The number of indictable offences known to the police in England and Wales in 1955 was 438,085, a fall of 5.1 per cent over the previous five years. Five years later, the figure was 743,713, a massive increase of 64.4 per cent. Looked at another way, 11,234 offences per million people in 1955 rose to 18,471 per million in 1960. The rise was startling. Violent crime had doubled; theft and other crimes against property were up 72 per cent; sexual offences rose by 16.7 per cent.

In part, there was more theft because there was far more to steal and it was easier to do so. Open plan shops and supermarkets were a temptation to the light-fingered, where the old counter separating the customer from the goods had acted as a physical barrier to shoplifters. Likewise, more cars on the road meant more opportunities for car thieves. It was also much easier to offload stolen vehicles than when cars had been rarer and therefore more traceable. The same was true of house break-ins to steal new mod-cons, such as televisions and gramophones.

> '**I do not think that men are more sinful-hearted than they were. They are, however, I should say, more dangerously placed.**'
>
> Geoffrey Fisher, Archbishop of Canterbury

The rise in violence was less glibly accounted for. When Bill Haley and the Comets brought rock-and-roll to British cinemas in *Rock Around The Clock*, young Teddy Boys and others began ripping up the seats. 'Teenagers' were a 1950s phenomenon. Nobody had bothered with adolescents much when they had short hair, little money and did what they were told. Now they had attitude, and full employment gave them pockets deep enough to spend millions on clothes and records.

The Teds seemed designed to provoke their parents' generation. They liked to 'rumble', fighting in dancehalls and seaside resorts. One rampage through South London in 1956 left shop windows smashed and cars overturned. This was the first wide-scale hooliganism seen in the century. The Archbishop of Canterbury, Geoffrey Fisher, sought reasons for the rise in crime. 'Many of the time-honoured defences against bad thinking and bad-doing are weakened', he explained. 'Also the incentives to good thinking and good doing are less powerful than they were. There is, or may be, a loss of spiritual capital.'

A different morality

Children had always been allowed some licence, but within limits. Alan Titchmarsh, growing up in Yorkshire, remembered the night before Bonfire Night in his memoir *Nobbut A Lad*. It was called 'Mischief Night'. He and his friends

poured Lyle's golden syrup into a bit of greaseproof paper. They smeared this onto a front door handle, then knocked on the door and ran off to hide. The irritated householder would be left wiping his sticky palms and shouting 'little buggers' after them. The other trick was throwing metal dustbin lids as hard as they could into peoples' backyards. Young Titchmarsh got caught once, by Wilf Phillips, a neighbour who turned out to be a swift runner, even in carpet slippers. The boy got a clip round the ear, but it didn't occur to anyone to arrest Mr Phillips for assault or child abuse. The only criticism was that he couldn't take a joke, but as the children left him alone after that, he might be said to have had the last laugh.

Standards were beginning to change. Before long, it would not be so readily accepted that an adult had the right to tell off any child or youth. The battle between a person's rights and responsibilities was under way; rights were in the ascendant, but modestly so, for now.

Official morality took time to change. Princess Margaret could not in 1955 marry a divorced commoner, even one with so distinguished a war record as Group Captain Peter Townsend. The grandly titled League of Decency complained about hoardings showing Marilyn Monroe with her skirt billowing above her knees on adverts for *The Seven-Year Itch*. The offending posters were removed. In September 1957, the Wolfenden Report concluded that homosexual acts between consenting adults should be legalised. The government refused to accept its recommendations.

What R A Butler called 'Victorian corsetry' was loosened a little by the Obscene Publications Act of 1959. This led to a landmark case at the Old Bailey in

THE SQUARE MILE
Brokers and jobbers mingle in the 'Gorgonzola Hall' at the London Stock Exchange in Throgmorton Street in 1951. (The nickname comes from the greenish marble lining the hall, which someone decided resembled the famous green-veined Italian cheese.) The people and practices in the City appeared arcane to outsiders, but it was a foreign exchange earner of the first order and the centre of the world insurance markets. Although it might have seemed that New York's Wall Street would crush it as a global financial player, beneath the top hats, wing collars and grey hair there was a wealth of experience and a taste for innovation that would see the City survive and prosper.

1960 – the same year that the Commons voted against the legalisation of homosexuality – in which Penguin Books was charged with obscenity for publishing D H Lawrence's novel *Lady Chatterley's Lover*. The trial pitted the guardian of public morality, the Lord Chamberlain – in person, an earl and former Governor of Bombay – against the son of a Nottinghamshire miner. The prosecution not only held the book to be obscene, but also suggested that the plot itself – in which the 'lady of a great house', Lady Chatterley, was seen to 'run off and copulate with her husband's gamekeeper' – was somehow socially unnatural.

The trial had two particular high points. One was when the prosecuting counsel, Mervyn Griffith-Jones, showed how far the Establishment was adrift of the times when he asked the jury: 'Is it a book that you would wish your wife or servant to read?' The other was when Richard Hoggart was asked whether an obscenity gained anything from being written as asterisks, ****, rather than being spelled out. 'Yes', he said, in a flash, 'it gains a dirty suggestiveness.' The critic Kenneth Tynan said of the trial that it was the moment when the Old England of the prosecution and the cuckolded baronet, a place of 'separation ... control ... death', met in mortal combat with the 'contact ... freedom ... love' of Lawrence's brave New Britain. The new won the case. The book – ironically, now thought to be perhaps the worst of Lawrence's novels – sold out its first print-run of 200,000.

A NEW STYLE OF WRITING

Better, much better, books and plays were being written in the 1950s. It was the era of writers from 'redbrick' universities, so called because the newer provincial foundations lacked the mellow stones of Oxbridge. Two of the best, the novelist Kingsley Amis and poet Philip Larkin, had in fact met as students at Oxford. Larkin had gone on to become librarian at the University of Hull. Amis lectured at Swansea. Amis was from the South London suburbs and felt himself a victim of the 'constant anxieties over decorum' of the middle classes. These, he asserted, denied him the pleasures of either the working or upper classes – 'teenage sex behind a coal tip' for the one, and a 'fructifyingly bad time at Eton' for the other.

Amis's classic novel, *Lucky Jim*, was published in 1955. The hero was Jim Dixon, one of the great figures of English comic literature, a chaotic, put-upon and accident-prone lecturer at a provincial university, bored witless by his special subject – medieval shipbuilding – though his own ribaldry and liveliness had a medieval, or at least Chaucerian flavour. Dixon was a middle class anti-hero, waving two rude fingers to the literary elite and all it stood for.

'If you can't annoy somebody', Amis said, 'there's little point in writing.' And he succeeded triumphantly. The established but now fading Somerset Maugham thought Lucky Jim pinned down exactly the 'white collar proletariat', which was

continued on page 122

WRITERS

THE WORDSMITHS

The best writers, like Ian Fleming (top left) and J R Tolkien (top right) would eventually keep the film industry as well as publishers in plenty. Fleming began writing his first James Bond novel, *Casino Royale*, in 1952. He thought of his Bond books as 'pillow fantasy ... bang, bang, bang, kiss, kiss, that sort of stuff'. But that was why the public loved them. Tolkien is seen here in his study at Merton College, Oxford, shortly after the publication of the three-volume *The Lord of the Rings* in 1954-5. He was Professor of Anglo-Saxon and then of English Language and Literature at Oxford. His fascination with ancient sagas led him to create a world of his own, whose strange creatures eventually became the stars of three blockbuster films.

The poet Dylan Thomas (top centre), seen here in 1950, glass in hand as ever, destroyed himself and his wondrous talent with drink. Works like *Under Milk Wood*, his play for voices, had a rhythm and beauty that he caught best himself in his readings. He was dead, a savage literary loss, by 1953.

The novelist Christopher Isherwood (left, on left) is shown talking with Aldous Huxley in 1954. Isherwood was best-known for catching the spirit of 1930s Berlin in *Mr Norris Changes Trains* and *Goodbye to Berlin*. Huxley had recently experimented with the hallucinatory drug mescalin to explore mysticism in *The Doors of Perception*.

The poet John Betjeman, seen here outside his home in 1956 (bottom left), caught the snobberies and affectations of the age. In his poem 'How to Get On in Society', he mercilessly lampooned middle-class pretensions:

Phone for the fish-knives, Norman,
As Cook is a little unnerved;
You kiddies have crumpled the serviettes,
And I must have things daintily served.

Kingsley Amis (left) is seen enjoying a drink at a bar in Swansea in 1958. Drink was the undoing of the hero of his comic masterpiece, *Lucky Jim*, a wonderfully observed slice of life in a provincial university.

CREATIVE GENIUS

The artistic brilliance of the age is caught in this casual snap of film director Carol Reed (on the left, below) with the novelist Graham Greene in 1951. Reed was one of the world's best film directors, and Greene one of the finest writers. Reed had recently filmed Greene's script to make *The Third Man*, a masterly evocation of the sinister seediness of bombed-out post-war Vienna and its black marketeers, with Orson Welles magnificent as the penicillin profiteering Harry Lime.

MUSICIANS

Rock-and-roll could look after itself, but it was the BBC and the licence fee that kept classical music afloat. The highbrow Third Programme aired concerts and recitals, and the BBC had its own Symphony Orchestra, its Philharmonic Orchestra, a lighter Concert Orchestra, a Theatre Orchestra, a Northern Symphony Orchestra, a West of England Light Orchestra … As late as 1980, it still had eleven classical orchestras.

STIRRING PERFORMANCE
Sir Adrian Boult is seen here (left) conducting Michael Tippett's Second Symphony, commissioned by the BBC in 1958, as Tippett looks on. As a pacifist, Tippett had been briefly imprisoned during the war, but he had recovered to become a leading composer. His 1952 opera *The Midsummer Marriage* was a great success, and he followed it with a piano concerto and sonatas, and another opera, *King Priam*.

DYNAMIC DUO
The conductor and composer Benjamin Britten (at the piano) accompanies the violinist Yehudi Menuhin in 1955. Britten's best compositions in the 1950s were the opera *Billy Budd* and *Noye's Fludde*, a musical rendition of a medieval miracle play. Menuhin, born in New York, settled in England after the war and became a favourite with audiences.

BOND GIRL
The cellist Amaryllis Fleming (right) plays a solo at her 1953 debut at 'the Proms', the annual Promenade Concerts at the Albert Hall. She was the daughter of the artist Augustus John and Eve Fleming, who became John's mistress some time after the death of her husband. Eve was also the mother of travel writer Peter Fleming and his brother Ian, creator of James Bond. In a Bond short story, Fleming wrote of 'that girl Amaryllis somebody' with 'something almost indecent in the idea of that bulbous, ungainly instrument between her splayed thighs.' Amaryllis later became a Professor at the Royal College of Music.

ARTISTS & SCULPTORS

THE PLASTIC ARTS

Elisabeth Frink, at work in 1954 (main picture), was known for her animal subjects, birds, dogs, shepherds and their sheep, and her series of horse and rider sculptures. Her work often had a coiled and menacing quality, achieved by using a scarred and distressed surface. The sculptor Henry Moore (right) examines his latest work, an upright exterior-and-interior form, in his studio at Perry Green in Hertfordshire.

Augustus John (left) works on a sculpture in 1956. He was famous for his paintings of gipsies and fishermen, and for his portraits of striking women. He was the father of a future Sea Lord, and of the concert cellist Amaryllis Fleming.

Stanley Spencer (left, below) in 1956, painting 'Dinner on the Hotel Lawn', one of a series of paintings he made on the regatta at Cookham, the Thames-side village where he lived. Spencer was a well-loved eccentric, who also painted deeply unfashionable religious subjects.

Jacob Epstein stands next to his sculpture of Lucifer at an exhibition in London in 1952 (right, below). Epstein modelled the heads of famous men – Einstein, Joseph Conrad, George Bernard Shaw – but his later primitivist sculptures, like Adam, caused uproar and accusations of obscenity.

'mean, malicious and envious', some of whom would take to drink, others to crime, but others would become 'schoolmasters and form the young, or journalists and mould public opinion'. A few, he said, would go on to become cabinet ministers and rule the country. Maugham thought himself fortunate that 'I shall not live to see it'. In fact, Dixon had no time for anyone, provincial or otherwise, attacking even at this very early stage 'the organic husbandry crowd', as well as potters, Esperanto-speakers and other would-be trend setters.

Angry young men

Another raw writing talent surfaced at the Royal Court Theatre in London's Sloane Square. The English Stage Company based there had several young actors of quality, including Alan Bates, Robert Stephens and Joan Plowright. The director Tony Richardson cut his teeth at the theatre under impresario George Devine. They badly needed a hit and ploughed through more than 700 scripts looking for a gem. They found it in a play written by a poverty-stricken young journalist and repertory actor, John Osborne, who was living on a houseboat in Chiswick. They paid him a £25 option, named his play *Look Back In Anger*, and staged it at the Royal Court in May 1956.

The critics – though not yet theatre audiences – were tiring of well-crafted, well-mannered plays in the style of Terence Rattigan or Noel Coward. In particular, they had their fangs into Rattigan. His 1954 play *Separate Tables* ran for 700 performances. This was not quite in the same league as Agatha Christie's *The Mousetrap*, which opened in October 1952 and is running to this day, but Rattigan had been going since before the war and familiarity had bred a certain

LOOKING FORWARD IN THEATRE
The 'angry young man' tag coincided with John Osborne's play *Look Back In Anger*, which had its premiere at the Royal Court Theatre in London in May 1955. The tangled lives of its young characters were a brutal break with traditional drawing-room theatre. It brought a new generation of British actors to the fore, including Alan Bates as the central character of Jimmy Porter, seen here with Kenneth Haigh (left) and Mary Ure.

contempt. He laid himself open to it by saying that he was writing for 'Aunt Edna', a nice, respectable, middle-aged maiden lady, a 'hopeless lowbrow' who lived in a Kensington hotel.

Fierce young Kenneth Tynan, who became theatre critic of *The Observer* when still in his 20s, used Aunt Edna to lampoon Rattigan mercilessly, putting her in conversation with a Young Perfectionist, who concluded that though there was something for everyone in a Rattigan work, there was not enough for anyone. Tynan fell upon Osborne's play with rapture. *Look Back In Anger* was set in a dreary one-room flat in the Midlands, and covered the tangled relations between a cynical and disaffected young man, Jimmy Porter, his wife, an army officer's daughter, her haughty best friend, and an affable Welsh lodger. Many found the play disturbing. One critic railed that the setting was 'unspeakably dirty and squalid. It is difficult to believe that a colonel's daughter, brought up with some standards, would have stayed in this sty for a day.' That, though, was why Tynan so admired it. It was gritty, he thought, and true.

The play was, in fact, largely based on Osborne's own unhappy marriage and life in a cramped flat in Derby. It 'presents post-war youth as it really is', Tynan said, 'the drift towards anarchy, the instinctive leftishness, the automatic rejection of "official" attitudes, the casual promiscuity …' He agreed that the play was a minority taste, but it was a minority 'of 6,733,000, which is the number of people in this country between 10 and 30'. He concluded by saying: 'I doubt if I could love anybody who did not wish to see *Look Back In Anger*.' It was an extraordinary review, and it helped to open the floodgates.

The writer Allan Sillitoe said Osborne did not contribute to the British theatre, 'he set off a landmine and blew most of it up'. The *Daily Express* coined the phrase 'angry young men' a few months later.

The 'genius' outsider

The phrase was instantly applied to the author of *The Outsider*, an unlikely bestseller that was published within a fortnight of the opening of Osborne's play. It was written by Colin Wilson, a former laboratory assistant, steel plant worker, hospital porter and self-confessed 'genius', who had left school in Leicester at 16. Wilson lived in a sleeping bag on Hampstead Heath by night. By day, after a bus ride from the Heath and a stop at a busmen's cafe for a cup of tea, he wrote a long, often unintelligible philosophical ramble in the Reading Room of the British Museum, which quoted, seemingly at random, every intellectual from Kierkegaard to Nietzsche and Schopenhauer. He called the book *The Outsider*, after the work by Albert Camus, reflecting his interest in French existentialism.

The genius lay in the timing. Philosophy and the romantic figure of the alienated thinker darted briefly into fashion in the 1950s. The book itself made little sense, but this in a way was a virtue, for it spared people the effort of reading it and it mentioned every intellectual they had ever heard of. Reviews sold books as well as plays, and Wilson's were astonishing. *The Observer* called *The Outsider* a 'luminously intelligent study of a representative theme of our time'. The *Daily Mail* critic wrote breathlessly: 'I have just met my first genius. His name is Colin Wilson.' The *Daily Express* commissioned him to write a piece as an angry young man. 'I wasn't in the least angry', Wilson said later. 'Being the author of a best-seller was certainly better than working in a factory.' But the *Express* money was good, though he complained that, with all the attention he was getting,

STALLS OR CIRCLE
The year before John Osborne's stage bombshell, a theatre-goer buys tickets at Preston theatre to see a revue called *All Shapes and Surprises*, staged by actor-manager Terry Cantor. The more traditional plays and stage shows would continue to have their appeal.

'my life turned into a sort of gossip column'. For a time, the papers were full of him, particularly when his girlfriend's father found one of his notebooks for a future novel, full of what he took to be pornography. He burst into Wilson's flat, brandishing a horsewhip, and shouting: 'Aha, Wilson, the game is up! We know what's in your filthy diary.'

The 'angry' tag was also applied to a new wave of working class writers, and their 'gritty realism', much of it based in the Midlands and North. Sillitoe himself was among them. The anti-hero of his novel *Saturday Night and Sunday Morning* was Arthur Seaton, a young lathe operator in a Nottingham bicycle factory. His ambition went no further than 'a good life: plenty of work and plenty of booze and a piece of skirt every month until I'm 90'. It was part autobiographical. Sillitoe had worked in the Raleigh bicycle factory after leaving school at 14. The novel was turned into a successful film. *Look Back In Anger* was, too, with Richard Burton cast as Jimmy Porter.

The new writers pumped fresh blood into the cinema. Keith Waterhouse was a greengrocer's son from Hunslett in Leeds, who had left school at 15 to work in a cobbler's shop. He took a day in the life of Billy Fisher, an incorrigible fibber juggling with the affections of three girls, for his whimsical novel *Billy Liar*. It was turned into a play with Albert Finney in the lead, then a film with Tom Courtenay and Julie Christie, directed by John Schlesinger, later an Oscar winner.

Another Yorkshireman, John Braine, had a best-selling novel that turned into a hit film with *Room At The Top*. Like Sillitoe, Braine had taken to writing while convalescing from tuberculosis. Braine's anti-hero was Joe Lampton, proud of his working class roots but ruthlessly determined to leave them as far behind as he could. Lampton was driven by the materialism that was to become so entrenched. He sees the Yorkshire town where he is on the make not as buildings and landscape, but as shops and aspirational goods: 'Finlay the tailor with Daks and Vantella shirts and Jaeger dressing gowns, Robbins the chemist with the bottles of

ROOM AT THE TOP
The quality of British film had seldom been higher. A stream of plays and novels were turned into gritty, realist films, with a fresh focus on working class heroes and heroines set in the industrial North and Midlands. Simone Signoret and Laurence Harvey are seen here in *Room at the Top*, taken from John Braine's bestselling portrait of a cynical and amoral young Yorkshireman on the make.

Lentheric after-shave lotion ...' The author himself could now afford to shop in them. The book earned Braine £10,000 in the first two months after its publication in 1957, a far cry from the £600 a year he was earning as a librarian in Wakefield. The 'angry young man' tag was applied to Braine as well but, like the others, he said he was not in the least angry. 'What I want to do', he said, 'is to drive through Bradford in a Rolls-Royce with two naked women on either side of me covered in jewels.'

Shelagh Delaney was the leading woman writer from the provincial working class. She left school in Salford at 16 and worked in a factory and as an usherette while writing her first play, *A Taste of Honey*. It was anchored in the shabby streets of Manchester and centred on Jo, with her drinking, loose-living mother, gay employer and black lover. Joan Littlewood took it for the experimental Theatre Workshop in East London in 1958 and struck a chord. It transferred to the West End then to Broadway, and was made into an award-winning film by Tony Richardson.

The London dramas of Arnold Wesker were even more 'kitchen sink'. The son of Jewish immigrants who started out as a plumber's mate, Wesker wrote a trilogy on the struggles of the Kahn family between 1958 and 1960; *Chicken Soup with Barley* was the best known of them. Harold Pinter was another play-writing talent to emerge from an East End Jewish family.

Actors were also changing from the exquisitely mannered old school of the likes of Ralph Richardson and John Gielgud. Now, actors valued their provincial or working-class backgrounds. Albert Finney was from Salford, Tom Courtenay from Hull, Peter O'Toole from Leeds, and Michael Caine, born Maurice Micklewhite, was the son of a fish porter from Rotherhithe in southeast London.

The play that most brilliantly caught the post-Suez transformation in Britain was John Osborne's *The Entertainer*. He wrote it for Laurence Olivier, the country's finest actor, who wanted a fresh challenge after playing Shakespeare too often. Osborne cast him as Archie Rice, a gap-toothed music-hall artist in a seedy seaside resort, the embodiment of a class-ridden and moribund Establishment – Osborne called the monarchy 'the gold filling in a mouth of decay' – with a bickering, acrid family. As Archie went through his tired old gags and routines, his son Mick, killed in the Suez landings, symbolised the nation and an empire in its death throes. 'Don't clap too loud', Archie told his audience. 'This is a very old building.'

DECLINE AND FALL
Laurence Olivier rehearsing his role as Archie Rice, an ageing music-hall artist, in John Osborne's *The Entertainer*. The play was staged like a music hall evening, with different turns and sketches, and was a complete contrast to Olivier's usual stage roles. As the most acclaimed actor of his generation, Olivier was theatrical royalty, and he rose to the challenge to give a magnificent performance.

WIND OF
CHANGE

Developments in the arts and theatre in the latter
half of the 1950s had resonance with high politics.
Macmillan was himself seen as 'the Entertainer',
a faded relic of Edwardian splendour. In many
ways, though, he was very much in touch with his
time. The days of Empire were gone, and he was
doing his bit to send it on its way.

WORK AND PLAY Children in Yorkshire play on swings within sight of the factories where their fathers work.

MACMILLAN WINS AGAIN

Although some nations – India, Burma, Ceylon – had gained independence in the late 1940s, the British Empire was still a grand enterprise when Macmillan inherited it from Eden. In 1957, no fewer than 45 different countries were still governed by the Colonial Office in London. Within a few years, however, beginning with Ghana and Malaya, the major countries became independent. By the early 1960s Nigeria, Jamaica, Uganda, Tanganyika, Kenya, Zanzibar, Cyprus and others had all gone, including several where British soldiers had recently served.

In Tanganyika and Uganda, independence came faster than even the nationalist leaders expected – or indeed wanted. The results, in Uganda at least, were to prove catastrophic. In the words of the historian J R Seeley, the Empire was let go, much as it had been obtained, in a 'fit of absence of mind'.

'Are the people ready for self-government?' Macmillan asked the governor-general of Nigeria.

'No, of course not', came the reply.

'Then I said', Macmillan recalled, '"What do you recommend me to do?"'

The governor-general responded, 'I recommend you to give it to them at once'.

The Prime Minister himself had little interest in the colonies, beyond a vague dislike of the white settlers, whom he said reminded him of 'retired colonels in the golf club and their ladies'. He had never been to sub-Saharan Africa when he became prime minister in 1956. When he did go, to Cape Town early in 1960, he made his famous and resonant 'wind of change' speech that heralded majority rule for all the former British colonies on the African continent.

> The Empire was let go, much as it had been obtained, in a 'fit of absence of mind'.

HE'D NEVER HAD IT SO GOOD
Harold Macmillan and his wife, Lady Dorothy, during his election triumph of 1959. His first seat was for Stockton-on-Tees, but he had moved to a safer one in Bromley after the war. It was the third Conservative victory in a row and they increased their majority to more than 100 seats, after a lacklustre performance by Labour under Hugh Gaitskill. The Tories under Macmillan were dogma-free and pragmatic. Asked what the greatest challenge for a statesman was, Macmillan replied: 'Events, dear boy, events.'

FRUITS OF EMPIRE
The national taste for brown sauce, here the O.K brand, originated with fruits shipped in from the old empire. Oranges and grapes came from South Africa, apples from New Zealand, apricots from Australia. These had been luxuries during rationing, sold at high prices by 'barrow boys', close relations to spivs and black marketeers. Now they arrived in increasing volume and at lower prices. The Empire provided wine, too, though the art of fine winemaking had yet to reach the southern hemisphere, and the rough taste of South African or Australian sherry was not for those with refined palettes.

After the 1959 election, Macmillan appointed Iain Macleod as colonial secretary. Macleod was a brilliant gambler and card player; he had played bridge for England in his early 20s and made a large tax-free income from gaming. He had so little interest in the colonies, he had never actually set foot in one. The British themselves thought of the white dominions – Australia, Canada, New Zealand – almost as extensions of the mother country. They were largely indifferent to the rest. The Empire meant food more than anything. Lamb and butter from New Zealand, Australian beef and tinned apricots, Nigerian and Gold Coast cocoa, Kenyan coffee, West Indian rum and Demerara sugar and treacle, Cyprus sherry and other 'Empire wines' were staples.

It was through the explosion of Chinese and Indian restaurants that immigrant Britain was most visible. Curry was hardly a new dish. Mrs Beeton had included 14 curry recipes in her household-management book of 1859, and before the Second World War there were Taj Mahals and Kohinoors to be found in several cities. Now, curry houses were reaching even medium-sized towns. Then in 1958 John Koon, who ran the upmarket Lotus House restaurant in Soho, came up with an innovation: he borrowed the fish-and-chips idea and opened the first Chinese takeaway in London's Queensway.

By the end of the decade, the black and Asian population in Britain had reached 337,000 in a total population of around 50 million. Soon, the equivalent of the total non-white population of 1951 would be arriving every two years. It was the largest mass immigration in British history. Many arrived in response to recruitment drives by British employers, but in any case they were entitled to come as British citizens. The Nationality Act of 1948 had granted all subjects of the colonies and Commonwealth the right to come to the 'mother country' to live and work. (Britain in the 1950s had no immigration controls. The government introduced the first, the Commonwealth Immigration Act, in 1961 following a sharp rise in numbers the previous year.)

The shock of race riots

In 1958, Britain experienced its first race riots. They came as something of a shock to a country that saw itself as more enlightened than, say, South Africa or the American South. It would prove to be a watershed in race relations.

West Indians in London had clustered in Brixton and in Notting Hill, working-class, inner-city areas with problems of decaying housing, in a post-war Britain with a severe housing shortage. Many landlords were unwilling to let to new immigrants; rooms advertised for rent would suddenly be 'already taken'. Others took advantage by charging higher rents to black tenants, cramming 20 people or more into a single Victorian house. The notorious slum landlord Peter Rachman even bullied white residents into leaving, with threats, filth pushed through letter boxes, roofs opened to the rain, so he could rent out for more money to people desperate for a place to live. The first immigrants to move in were single young men (West Indian women generally did not arrive in significant numbers until a bit later in the decade) and they followed very different lifestyles to their white neighbours. They sat around outside on the streets, talking loudly and playing the West Indian music that they had brought with them. Tensions rose, with KBW, Keep Britain White, scrawled on walls.

Yet it was not London but Nottingham that saw the first outright riot, and it was not sparked by the housing crisis but by a black man talking to a white

INDEPENDENCE DAYS

LET MY PEOPLE GO

Independence was gathering speed across the Empire. In West Africa, the Duchess of Kent (above) reads a message from the Queen in 1957. It grants independence to the people of the Gold Coast, which became Ghana. The scene is the National Assembly in Accra, capital of the new Ghana. The old trade links remained. The cocoa bean still underpinned the Ghanaian economy, the vital ingredient in Britain's chocolate bars and nightcap cup of cocoa.

The Duke of Gloucester played the same role the same year in Kuala Lumpur (left) for the Malayan Proclamation of Independence. The Paramount Ruler, the Yang Di-Pertuan Agong (centre) and Tunku Abdul Rahman (right), share the dais with him. There was a particular poignancy. British and Commonwealth troops had fought long and hard to combat the communist insurgency in Malaya. This ceremony, and the orderly handover of power, was the legacy they left.

HARD STRUGGLE

TRAGEDY OF INTOLERANCE

The police move in to arrest white youths during the riots of September 1958 (above). West Indian immigrants had not expected the prejudice they met when they arrived to work in Britain, the 'mother country'. But some met with much worse. Kelso Cochrane had arrived from Antigua in 1954 and was working as a carpenter while he saved up to study law. On 17 May, 1959, he was stabbed to death by a gang of white youths near his home in Notting Hill. The murder inspired demonstrations (left) and became national news. More than 1200 people, black and white, attended Cochrane's funeral. The police interviewed more than 900 people in the investigation and insisted that the motive was robbery, but they found insufficient evidence to charge anyone. To this day, no-one has been prosecuted for what many believe was Britain's first racist black murder.

woman in a pub in St Ann's. The ensuing fight spilled outdoors and seven white men needed hospital treatment. An angry white crowd soon gathered, armed with bottles and razors, and set off through the streets, attacking any unfortunate lone immigrant who happened to be in the wrong place at the wrong time.

Events in Notting Hill had a similar start. Over and above the belief that immigrants were taking houses and jobs away from the British, it seems what white English men found hardest to handle was the thought of black men having any sort of relationship with white women. A Swedish woman who was married to an immigrant was attacked by a white gang in Notting Hill, and had to be escorted to her home by police. As in Nottingham, this was the spark for mobs of angry young white men to run riot, attacking any vulnerable immigrants they came across. Most people, black and white, stayed indoors in the evenings when the violence was at its worst, but not all West Indians were prepared to keep their heads down. Some retaliated and running fights between black and white gangs went on for several days. A great tropical downpour on the night of 5 September finally broke the cycle. As the dust settled, many began to question their own attitudes and those of society as a whole towards the question of race and prejudice. Legislation to outlaw discrimination was still well in the future, but the seeds had been sown that would lead to a more tolerant Britain.

The H-Bomb and Cold War Spies

More peaceable were the mass demonstrations against 'the Bomb'. Kingsley Amis said in 1957 that there were no great causes left, 'no Spain, no Fascism, no mass unemployment'. It was difficult for the intellectual rebel to become passionate about strikes, he said, when strike pay was as much as he got himself 'for a review of Evelyn Waugh or a talk about basset-horns on the Third Programme'. He was about to be proved wrong. The first test explosion of a British H-bomb in the megaton range took place at Christmas Island in November 1957. Protests, and demands to 'Ban the Bomb', had taken time to get going. When CND, the Campaign for Nuclear Disarmament, did get under way, it remained a fixture for many years. Some people had found their new great cause.

Cold War tensions and spy fevers were thriving. Agents and double agents existed in the flesh as well as in the latest James Bond fiction. A headless body believed to be that of the frogman Buster Crabb was found in Chichester harbour in June 1957. Crabb had disappeared while diving near a Red Navy cruiser that had brought the Soviet leaders Nikolai Bulganin and Nikita Khrushchev to Portsmouth on their visit a year before. Crabb was presumed to have been on a mission for British intelligence to examine the cruiser's hull.

The most renowned spies of the decade, though, were the Foreign Office traitors Guy Burgess and Donald Maclean. 'B and M', as the press called them, reappeared in Moscow in 1956 after vanishing from Britain five years earlier. They fled after being been tipped off by a 'third man' that MI5 and Special Branch were on to them. That man was later discovered to be Kim Philby, another pro-Communist traitor, who also duly popped up in Moscow. It later came out that

> The most renowned spies of the decade ... were Foreign Office traitors Guy Burgess and Donald Maclean.

THE MISSING FROGMAN

The diver Lionel 'Buster' Crabb is seen here telling a group of admiring children tales of derring-do at Tobermory on the Isle of Mull. Crabb was a Second World War hero. He had won the George Cross for dealing with limpet mines attached to ships by enemy frogmen, and for clearing Italian ports of mines and bombs. He was on the verge of retirement when he dived in Portsmouth harbour on 19 April, 1956. He was almost certainly working for British intelligence, and had been sent to examine the hull of the Soviet cruiser that brought Nikolai Bulganin and Nikita Khrushchev to Britain on an official visit. Crabb was never seen alive again. A body, thought to be Crabb's, was later found in a frogman's suit at Pilsey Island in Chichester Harbour. The head and hands were missing, so it was impossible to identify him beyond doubt. It was one of the great mysteries of the decade.

COLD WAR TRAITOR

Seeming confident and self-assured, the intelligence officer Kim Philby (left) holds a press conference in November 1955, having been cleared of spying for the Soviet Union. Two of his former Foreign Office colleagues, Burgess and Maclean, had vanished in 1951. They had disappeared after being tipped off by a so-called 'third man' that MI5 had found out they were Soviet spies. Philby successfully denied that he was that man. He left the intelligence service and worked as a journalist in Beirut from 1956 – the same year that Burgess and Maclean resurfaced in Moscow. In 1963, Philby also appeared in Moscow and admitted his past treachery.

there were two others involved, one of whom, Anthony Blunt, was knighted in 1956 for his work as Surveyor of the Queen's Pictures. He was named in 1979 and stripped of his honours.

The rise of CND

In times like these, Nye Bevan, shadow foreign secretary, and the Labour leadership felt it wrong for Britain alone to renounce nuclear weapons. 'Do not send me naked into the conference chamber', Bevan had appealed to delegates at the Labour Conference as he argued the case for the H-bomb. He was heckled in response. The swelling CND movement also begged to disagree.

CNDs leaders were from a different generation to its youthful rank-and-file. They included the venerable mathematician and philosopher Bertrand Russell, a veteran pacifist from the First World War. John Collins, canon of St Paul's, was clergyman-in-chief. J B Priestley, the novelist and playwright, author of *The Good Companions*, sparked things off with an article in the *New Statesman* in November 1957, describing how nuclear-armed Britain could be 'turned into a

BAN THE BOMB
The first British H-bomb in the megaton range was exploded at Christmas Island in November 1957. The following Easter rain-soaked members of CND, the new Campaign for Nuclear Disarmament, marched to the Atomic Weapons Establishment at Aldermaston. The CND symbol on a duffel coat or anorak became part of the dress code of many students.

radioactive cemetery'. Opponents found the logic faulty. How would Britain be safer if it could no longer retaliate in kind? A long-running argument was born.

On Good Friday 1958, the coldest Easter for 40 years, 4000 protesters met in Trafalgar Square, then marched to the Atomic Weapons Establishment at Aldermaston in Berkshire, sleeping overnight in church and village halls. This was a new style of protest. It was not backed by a political party. It had few staff. Its supporters were largely middle class, many of them women. The young, in typical beards, sandals and baggy sweaters, were paid most attention by the press, but the marchers came from all age groups. They wore CND badges, with a curious but instantly recognisable symbol. Its designer, Gerald Holton, was chairman of his local group of CND in the leafy London suburb of Twickenham. He had originally thought of a cross, because the first march took place at Easter, but Pat Arrowsmith, CND's more media-conscious secretary, thought this was inappropriate as the march was not religious. The final logo had a circle, representing an unborn child, around lines meant to represent a dying man and the semaphore positions for N, nuclear, and D, disarmament. It was simple and striking, and so was the marchers' slogan 'Ban the Bomb'.

The swept wings of Britain's V-bombers, which carried the H-bombs, were also distinctive. The first squadrons of Vulcans arrived at RAF airfields in

Lincolnshire in 1958, giving the marchers another venue to go to, in addition to Aldermaston, party conferences and Trafalgar Square, where they became a part of the national calendar of events. For all their energy, however, they had little impact on defence policy in Britain, and despite their touching belief in the international effect that a moral example by Britain could have, they had no impact at all where it mattered most – in Washington and Moscow.

SUMMER HOLIDAYS

HAPPY CAMPERS
Two girls catch a press photographer's eye at Butlin's Holiday Camp at Clacton in 1950. Billy Butlin was the king of the holiday camps, the stay-in-Britain package where entertainment, baby-sitting and fun and games were guaranteed. There was always something to do at Butlin's – like riding a bicycle made for two.

For some, life was too short to take so seriously. The British had a genius for package holidays, dating back to Thomas Cook in 1841, if not to the Prince Regent and the creation of resort towns like Brighton half a century before that. They pioneered the holiday camp, from whose lines of shed-like 'chalets' lined up by frigid North Sea beaches are derived the modern all-in resorts, set in tropical gardens and caressed by the warm waters of the Caribbean.

Billy Butlin was the mastermind. He had built his first camp in the 1930s at Skegness, on 200 acres of former turnip field, and never looked back. He turned

continued on page 142

IMAGES OF THE SEASIDE

Mass package holidays abroad were in their infancy, and there was something Spartan and stoical about the long rows of people who sat on often windswept British beaches, convinced that 'the sea air' was doing them good. Holiday camps apart, little had changed since Victorian days.

BRAVING THE BREEZE
Blackpool offered a big funfair and variety shows as well as a sandy but often chilly beach. Donkey rides were a traditional treat, more usually for younger riders than these girls (right), ambling slowly here beneath the outline of Blackpool Tower. As a landmark, the tower was as familiar to generations of northerners as its older and grander cousin, built by Gustave Eiffel, was to Parisians.

Britain's tidal beaches, like this one at Scarborough in North Yorkshire (left), were more fun for small children than the tideless Mediterranean. Armed with a bucket and spade, essential seaside accessories, hours of fun could be had digging holes and building sandcastles. This little girl's displays Mickey Mouse, an early example of Disney's awareness of the commercial value of the brand.

PUSHING THE BOAT OUT
A youngster gives his pal a push start in the land yacht *Genevieve* at St Annes on Sea in Lancashire. Best-known for its championship golf club, Royal Lytham & St Annes, it was also the venue for the International Sand Yacht Speed Trials, which inspired these boys. They built *Genevieve* from old pram wheels and spare parts, with a raincoat for a sail. Children were encouraged to be active, and the 'health and safety' culture, which would now doubtless condemn *Genevieve* out of hand for lack of brakes and failure to conform to EU standards, had not yet taken root.

WELL-EARNED REST
Less active on the beach were the grandparent generation, here dozing on the Isle of Wight. Retirement in the 1950s largely meant what it said: it was not an opportunity, as it is now, to take up bungee-jumping and exotic travel.

SEASIDE SNACKS
Fish and chips, and whelks and winkles, were as much a part of a day at the seaside as the flat cap and rolled up trousers, seen here at Scarborough on a bracing August day in 1952. Annual holidays were much shorter than today – most people had a fortnight a year or so at most – and many also had to work on Saturday mornings, so Bank Holidays were always eagerly looked forward to.

3/-
3/6
1/6
3/6
4/-
2/-
4/6
2/6
2/6
2/6
2/-

FRESH
PRAWNS
1/-

FRESH
SHRIMPS
6d
PER · BAG

WINKLES
6d
PER

MRS CO   KES
FISH   ALER

A LAUGH A MINUTE
Morning, noon and night, the Butlins Redcoats in their distinctive red blazers were entertaining their guests. The Redcoat here is supervising a 'knobbly knees' competition in 1955 at Skegness, Butlin's original camp.

the war to good account. He built three new camps and the government paid much of the cost because they wanted to use them for barracks. With peacetime, the shrewd showman got them back at a bargain price and filled them with holiday-makers. While rationing lasted, campers handed in their ration books at the beginning of their week, for the chef to clip for them. By the late Fifties, Butlin was running nine camps hosting 60,000 guests, known as 'campers', each week. He staged opera and Shakespeare in his camps, but the main entertainment fare were events and activities organised by the staff of Redcoats – bingo, ballroom dancing, cabarets, swimming and competitions for Finest Legs, Knobbly Knees, Baldest Head. Friday nights in the ballroom brought their fair share of mischief, but the Redcoats were always at hand to restore order.

The start of package tours

The Butlin's camps were hardly in exotic locations – Filey, Clacton, Bognor – but they were in effect all-in package tours without the airplane. Those were provided by another holiday pioneer, Vladimir Reitz, co-founder of Horizon Holidays. Reitz organised the first charter flights, from Gatwick to Corsica, in 1950. Two years later, he began package tours to Palma in Mallorca, extending them to the Costa Brava in 1954. It was the start of a process that was to transform the Spanish coastline, for better or worse. It would also change the holiday habits of the British nation, as the price of air-and-hotel deals in the sun became ever keener.

Two weeks in Majorca could be had for 39 guineas, and a further five guineas bought a tour of the Swiss Alps. Charging in guineas, the preserve of doctors, jewellers and bloodstock agents, was a sign of would-be sophistication – and a means of increasing the price by 5 per cent, a guinea being £1 1shilling (£1.05p). Some people were so worried at going abroad that they made wills before they left, explaining that they had never heard of going overseas 'except in a war'.

In truth, the British had been a 'low-bred amphibious mob' long before Daniel Defoe so described them. They had populated wildernesses from Virginia to Sydney, and some were tremendous travellers. Now they took to aircraft as they had in an earlier age taken to ships. Heathrow, a permanent building site then as now, was already Europe's premier airport, and overcrowded enough to keep Gatwick busy. The number of people going abroad more than doubled over the decade. It was an inescapable fact that, where garlic and olive trees flourished, so did sunshine. On the shores of the Mediterranean the sea ceased to be something to look at from behind a wind-break on a chilly pebble beach, and became a place to swim, frolic and get a suntan. But Billy Butlin still thrived for the moment, with his showman's flair and the British taste for communal holidays, a product of decades of works outings and Bank Holiday excursions.

Farewell to the seaside landlady

The resorts at home, and the seaside landlady, were the main casualties of 'abroad'. The landladies were a breed apart. Wielding rules and regulations, they chased families out at 10am sharp, into storms and rain scudding in from the Irish or North Sea, and did not let them back in until meal-times came round. They soldiered on in big resorts like Blackpool, close to the northern cities, and with a good Bank Holiday trade and big-name entertainers on the fairground. But for the less well-placed, it became a case of survival.

Hotels were hurt, too, and sought scapegoats in the press. The president of the Scarborough hoteliers, Harry Lund, railed at 'the garlic and olive oil gang of the press and radio'. Why, he asked, were bacon and eggs mocked in favour of Continental meals that were 'dollops of spaghetti with a little tomato sauce?' But even a big party of Derbyshire miners, who took a cook and their own beer with them to the Adriatic, admitted that 'wine and spaghetti are not all bad'.

> Some people were so worried at going abroad that they made wills before they left … they had never heard of going overseas 'except in a war'.

THE RISE AND RISE OF TELEVISION

If holidays abroad and living with the Bomb were 1950s novelties, so was television. This was the decade it came of age, undergoing a tremendous boom. Sets had got cheaper over the decade, but it still needed a real financial sacrifice to buy one. In 1958, a TV with a 17-inch tube cost 67 guineas (over £70) – five times the weekly wage for most, and a reason why many TVs were rented for 11 shillings (£0.55p) a week. By the end of the decade, 10 million sets were being watched each evening by roughly half the population. The number of combined radio and TV licences sailed past radio-only ones, and almost nine-tenths of the country was within range of both BBC and the new ITV transmitters.

Commercial television went on air for the first time on 22 September, 1955. The Hallé orchestra played, and speeches were shown from the launch banquet at the Guildhall. A variety show, excerpts from plays, a boxing match and an epilogue were rounded off by the National Anthem. Three two-minute advertising breaks an hour were permitted. The first-ever commercial, at 8.20pm, was for Gibbs SR toothpaste. The most popular programmes of the day were *Sunday Night at the London Palladium* hosted by Bruce Forsyth, *Take Your Pick* where Michael Miles would do his best to get contestants to say the little words 'Yes' or 'No', and Hughie Green's *Double Your Money*. Green's quiz show ran for 13

EXOTIC CREATURES

David Attenborough's *Zoo Quest* was a fine example of television that informed as well as entertained. Here, Prince Charles and Princess Anne meet the young naturalist in the BBC's Lime Grove Studios in 1958. Attenborough is introducing them to a cockatoo that he brought back from one of his expeditions to the world's wild places, filming rare wildlife in natural surroundings. His career was to span more than half a century, proof that quality could find a place on 'the box'.

years, and though it was attacked as mindless nonsense, he himself was an interesting man, a former Royal Canadian Air Force pilot and wheeler-dealer. The success of *The Army Game*, with Sergeant Major Bullimore trying to drill martial spirit into the feckless conscripts at Nether Hopping, reflected an audience in which practically everyone had some connection with military life.

The creation of *Coronation Street* was quirkily British. In the 1950s Tony Warren, a young actor-writer, was making £30 a week working for Granada TV, writing scripts on Biggles, the heroic airman of Captain W E Johns's flying yarns. But Warren's creative mind strayed far from the ace aviator to terraced streets and the wish to write 'something from the heart, acted by genuine Northerners'. One night was enough for him to write the first episode, complete with Elsie Tanner, Ken Barlow, Ena Sharples and the other classic early characters. When the idea came up for discussion at a Granada board meeting, the sales director thought it had no legs, but it squeezed through. With its name changed from Florizel Street to Coronation Street, it went on air in 1960 and became a legend.

A very British box

Television was much less affected by American imports than the cinema. Pan-European programmes had started with the first Eurovision Song Contest, held in

THE KING OF SKIFFLE
Skiffle was an eccentric, home-grown half-way house between rock and folk, played with an acoustic guitar, a washboard and a home-made tea-chest bass. By the time Lonnie Donegan and his band played at BBC's Twickenham studios for the *Six-Five Special* in 1957, they had moved on from amateur instruments and Lonnie (at the microphone) was the crowned king of skiffle. He got his break with the Chris Barber Jazz Band in the early 1950s, and his recording of *Rock Island Line*, made with Barber, not only went to No.1 in the UK but also reached the Top 10 in the USA. Between 1956 and 1962, Donegan had more than 20 hits. He was the first superstar of British pop and influenced many later musicians, including The Beatles.

1956 at Lugano, but generally 1950s television, like radio, was a very British affair. In children's programmes *The Adventures of Robin Hood*, starring Richard Greene, offered a medieval bows and arrows alternative to Hollywood cowboys and Indians. Billy Bunter ate away at Greyfriars School, dieting not being a fad in a country that had just come off rationing. The BBC had classic serials on Sunday afternoons of *The Railway Children*, *The Secret Garden* and the like.

Many programmes stimulated the imagination of the young. *Blue Peter* began in 1958. Any child with an interest in nature could watch Armand and Michaela Denis on safari in Africa. Hans and Lotte Hass took them diving and the deeper underwater world was revealed by Jacques Cousteau. Johnny Morris was at Bristol Zoo. The young David Attenborough, the most enduring creator of high-quality BBC programmes, started *Zoo Quest* in 1954.

TV starts to rock-and-rolll

It was the BBC, rather than ITV, that first saw the potential in television pop music. It began at the cost of the 'Toddler's Truce'. This was the shutdown of programmes between 6pm and 7pm, designed to get small children to go to bed without throwing tantrums about staying up to go on watching. ITV had lobbied to end this closure, as it cost them money from lost commercials, where the BBC, secure in the licence fee, lost nothing.

The BBC, though, made the most flamboyant use of the extra hour when the government agreed to relax the restriction, apart from Sundays when viewers were theoretically at, but in practice increasingly absent from, evensong in Church. From Mondays to Fridays, the BBC put on the news magazine *Tonight* in the new slot. But on Saturdays – starting on 16 February, 1957, the first post-truce evening – it began a new programme with live pop music and a live audience aimed at teenagers and the young. It came on after a news bulletin, and was called the *Six-Five Special* after its opening time.

It was introduced by Pete Murray, with a formula whose clichés were soon painfully dated, but were then the ultimate in teenage chic: 'Welcome aboard the *Six-Five Special*. We've got almost a hundred cats jumping here, some real cool characters to give us the gas, so just get on with it and have a ball.' Murray's co-presenter, Jo Douglas, then translated this for parents and 'all the squares' who were watching as: 'Just relax and catch the mood with us.' The first programme was played in by Kenny Baker and his Jazzmen. The show was only scheduled to run for six weeks, but it soon had an audience of 12 million with plenty of adults among the teenagers.

ITV soon poached the *Six-Five* producer, Jack Good, and launched its own Saturday evening, head-to-head rival show, *Oh Boy!* Not only the performers were young. Good and his script writer, Trevor Peacock, were 17 year olds, and the

'The 6.5 Special's steamin' down the line,
The 6.5 Special's right on time …
… My heart's a-beatin', 'cos I'll be meetin'
The 6.5 Special at the station tonight.'

POP IDOL
Tommy Steele performing at the Cat's
Whisker in London with Leon Bell and his
band in 1957. Steele was the first British
pop idol, though his best-selling records,
like *Singin' the Blues*, were covers of
American rock hits. Born Thomas Hicks,
and a former merchant sailor, Steele was
skilfully promoted by a canny agent, Larry
Parnes, whose stable of re-named rock
stars included Marty Wilde, Vince Eager and
Tommy Quickly. The most talented was
probably Billy Fury, whose lurid gold outfits
and exaggerated hip movements provided
valuable publicity by outraging the older
generation.

musical director, Harry Robinson was barely 24. Marty Wilde, born Reg Smith,
and Harry Webb from Hertfordshire, better known as Cliff Richard, were on
Oh Boy!'s first show. They were soon stars. So was Wee Willy Harris, a regular on
the programmes. He had bright blue hair, or green, or orange, depending on his
mood, and wore wide jackets, 'beetle crusher' shoes and a huge polka dot
bow tie. Jack Good discovered Terry Nelhams, a messenger boy from Acton,
who had started with a skiffle band and moved on to full-blooded rock-and-roll.
Good suggested a new name and a less aggressive, more boy-next-door style.
The new confection, now called Adam Faith, reached number one at Christmas
1959, with *What Do You Want*. The song was written by John Barry, an oddity
among rock musicians as the son of a classical pianist, who became a leading
composer of film scores.

There was still a strong market for ballads. The cane-carrying, top-hatted and
high kicking Frankie Vaughan sang *Kisses Sweeter Than Wine* and *Give Me the*

Moonlight. The West Indian pianist Winifred Atwell was a national favourite, the first black artist to sell a million records. She had trained at the Royal Academy of Music in London, and started her act playing a classical piece on a grand piano, before moving on to boogie-woogie on an old upright she had bought for 50 shilling (£2.50) from a Battersea junk shop.

Rock-and-roll is here to stay

Rock and pop were often written off. A critic compared Cliff Richard's eyeliner to that of film star Jayne Mansfield, and commented that if Cliff was acting naturally on *Oh Boy!* then 'consideration for medical treatment may be advisable'. But its defenders insisted that 'rock and roll is here to stay'. And so it proved. The first big rock manager was Larry Parnes, a former shopkeeper, who had a stable of stars including Billy Fury, Joe Brown and Marty Wilde. Tommy Steele was the first, though he had only one number one hit, *Singing the Blues* in 1957, and eventually went off to pursue a more traditional stage musical career.

Rock soon produced the first of its many nervous breakdowns. Terry Dene, a *Six-Five Special* hit with 'White Sport Coat', looked well on the way to stardom. His behaviour, though, was ahead of his time. The public was not yet used to pop stars trashing rooms and throwing tantrums when he was arrested for drunkenness and vandalism in 1958. The following year he was called up for his national service, but the barracks on the first day were too much for him. 'The thought of me in that little bed, with 15 other blokes all around', he said. 'I felt real sick. It was grim, man, grim.' Within 48 hours, he said, his psyche had collapsed. After two months in a psychiatric ward, the army let him return to his wife, the pop starlet Edna Savage. But when he reappeared on stage, men in the audience shouted at him to 'get back in the army'. His marriage failed. He turned to religion, becoming an evangelical street singer and recording gospel music.

Radio fights back

Despite the onslaught of TV, radio was enjoying a golden age. Since Sony launched the first transistor radio in 1956, almost everyone could afford one. Every day had a distinct pattern on radio. It started with the breakfast news, then moved onto *Housewives' Choice*. That was followed by *Music While You Work*. For children, *Listen With Mother* began at 1.45pm with the familiar refrain: 'Are you sitting comfortably? Then I'll begin.' *Mrs Dale's Diary* came on at teatime, followed at 5pm by *Children's Hour* with Uncle Mac.

Radio Newsreel was a part of the evening, with Wilfred Pickles and *Have A Go*, and its catchphrase 'Give him the money, Mabel'. *Educating Archie* with Peter Brough had the most bizarre star for radio, a ventriloquist's dummy. *Hancock's Half Hour* touched the same level of comic genius as *The Goons*, with Harry Secombe, Michael Bentine, Spike Milligan and Peter Sellers. In *Take It From Here* the Glum family got plenty of laughs through the bickering of Jimmy Edwards as Mr Glum with sweethearts Ron and Eth (Dick Bentley and June Whitefield).

The BBC was the most important patron of classical and light music in the country. It ran to over a dozen orchestras of one sort and another, and it was a huge employer of musicians. Most radio pop music listeners, though, tuned into a foreign commercial station, Radio Luxembourg, aimed specifically at teens.

continued on page 152

FAVOURITES ON RADIO

LISTENING IN

Winifred Atwell was a rarity: a classically trained pianist who played boogie-woogie and ragtime. Her signature tune, *Black and White Rag*, became a radio standard. She was the first black musician to sell a million records in Britain and is seen here in 1954 (left), celebrating the sale of her 5 millionth, with her allegedly music loving poodle. Born in Trinidad and Tobago, Atwell came to London to train at the Royal Academy of Music and was the first female pianist to win the Academy's highest grade for musicianship. She supported herself during her studies by playing ragtime in clubs and theatres. Eventually, she topped the bill at the London Palladium.

The Goon Show ran on the BBC Home Service from 1951 to 1960. The bow-tied actor Ian Carmichael joins the cast in this 1951 picture (right). From left are Spike Milligan, Peter Sellers, the bearded Michael Bentine and Harry Secombe. The show was a mixture of surreal humour, silly songs, awful puns and catch phrases, flung together with immense enthusiasm and bizarre sound effects. The Goons satirised all aspects of 1950s life, cocking a snook at business, trade unions, politicians, the army, police and much else, with Sellers and Milligan performing dozens of roles. It had a massive influence on comedy writing and still has a devoted fan base today.

Another brilliant comedy team were The Crazy Gang, appearing here (below) in *Knights of Madness* at the Victoria Palace Theatre in London. From the left they are: Jimmy Nervo, Teddy Knox, Bud Flanagan, Charlie Naughton and Jimmy Gold. Chesney Allen, one half of Flanagan and Allen, was also one of its stars. The Crazy Gang name was first used in 1937, but the component comedians had worked together before then, and continued on to give their last Royal Command Performance in 1967.

'We can't stand around here doing nothing. People will think we're workmen.'

Harry Secombe as Seagoon in The Goons

Cinema on the slide

The real loser in Britain's TV revolution was the cinema. It tried hard, even inventing its own 'English Marilyn Monroe' in Diana Dors, born Diana Fluck in Swindon in 1931. She gained invaluable publicity when the American censors demanded that her navel be covered in the film *Lady Godiva Rides Again*. She was the Variety Club's Personality of the Year, brash and bawdy and bottle blonde, an early Essex Girl. Neither she, though, nor brilliant films like *The Bridge on the River Kwai*, nor the valiant Carry On comedies that began with *Carry On Sergeant* in 1958, could turn the tide. It was a disastrous decade for Britain's cinemas, with a third of them, 1500 out of 4500, closing their doors for good or converting to bingo.

THE MAESTRO
The cinema slumped in terms of seats sold, but not in talent. Old masters like the director Alfred Hitchcock, seen here (above) filming *The Man Who Knew Too Much* in 1955, still found big audiences for his thrillers. Diana Fluck from Swindon, repackaged as Diana Dors, Britain's 'answer to Marilyn Monroe', kept the flag flying in the blonde bombshell stakes. She is seen here in 1958, at the wheel of her Cadillac convertible in front of her half-timbered 15th-century home in Sussex.

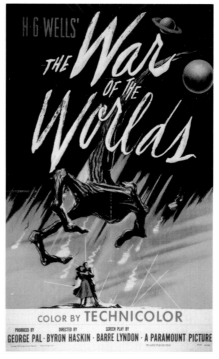

BRITISH BACKGROUNDS

The Scottish-born actress Deborah Kerr (left) starred as the British governess Anna Leonowens, with Yul Brynner as King Mongkut of Siam, in the hugely successful 1956 film *The King and I*. In her memoirs, Mrs Leonowens claimed that she had brought up the royal children in the 1860s, though in reality she seems to have been only their English teacher. *The War of the Worlds*, a 1953 film, was based on the 1898 science fiction novella by H G Wells, which told of the invasion of England by aliens from Mars. David Lean directed *The Bridge on the River Kwai*, an epic story of British prisoners of war working on the Burma Railway. Alec Guinness deservedly won an Oscar for his portrayal of the British commander. Here, he poses in front of the bridge, with William Holden (centre) and Jack Hawkins (right).

TEARS AND CHEERS

Football at the end of the decade was overshadowed by tragedy. Manchester United, the young 'Busby's babes' team, drew 3-3 in the quarter final of the European Cup against Red Star in Belgrade on 5 February, 1958. The next day, the BEA airliner bringing them home crashed on take-off from Munich after refuelling. Ice on the wings was initially blamed, but subsequent investigation showed slush build-up on the runway to be responsible. Twenty-three were killed, including eight players. Bobby Charlton, then just 20, survived the crash.

Britain won six gold medals in the Melbourne Olympics in 1956. Christopher Brasher won the 3000-metre steeplechase and there were other golds in boxing, women's fencing and backstroke. The equestrian events were held in Stockholm, because of Australian quarantine laws. The Queen was a part owner of Countryman, ridden by Bertie Hill, which was a member of the gold-winning Three Day Event team. It was some consolation for the Queen Mother's horse Devon Loch, which fell 50 yards from winning the Grand National.

Vanwall were the first Grand Prix team to win the Constructors Championship when it was held for the first time in the 1958 Grand Prix season. Vanwall brought together Stirling Moss, chassis maker Cooper Cars, Colin Chapman, later of Lotus, and businessman Tony Vandervell. As well as grand prix

TRAGEDY AND CELEBRATION
The ill-fated Manchester United team (below) before their quarter final against Red Star Belgrade in February 1958. They won on aggregate, but the team did not get the chance to fulfil its potential. Eight of the players were killed on the journey home when their chartered airliner crashed on its third attempt to take off from Munich.

Though he was never world champion, Stirling Moss was the greatest driver of his generation. He is seen here in 1955 (right) after becoming the first British driver to win the British Grand Prix, at the Aintree motor circuit. That same year he won the Mille Miglia, the Italian thousand-mile road race, finishing half an hour in front of Juan Manuel Fangio. Drivers worked much harder in those days. Moss competed in as many as 62 races a year. It was more dangerous, too. Moss retired after a near fatal crash in 1962.

RECORD-BREAKERS

QUICK, QUICK, SLOW

Donald Campbell, son of the pre-war land and water speed record-breaker Sir Malcolm Campbell, hurtles across Ullswater in Bluebird K7 in 1955 (top). He broke the 200mph barrier in July, and reached 216mph later in the year. By 1959, after beating his own records, he and Bluebird had reached 260mph.

A British pilot, Peter Twiss, broke the world air speed record in March 1956. He flew a Fairey Delta 2 at 1132mph, making it the first aircraft to exceed 1000mph in level flight. He is seen here a few weeks later (above right, on right) with the legendary American test pilot Chuck Yeager.

In contrast, the Antarctic explorer Vivian Fuchs and his Sno-Cat, seen here (above left) trekking across Antarctica in 1958, were not going to win any prizes for speed. But Polar exploration was in the blood of the nation that had produced Robert Falcon Scott and Ernest Shackleton.

victories, Stirling Moss won the Mille Miglia in Italy. The first British driver to win the world championship was Mike Hawthorn in 1958, although soon after he was killed on the Guildford by-pass when he crashed his racing-green Jaguar MK1.

Jaguar launched its MK1 in 1955, but the 100-mph Mk VII had been around since 1951. Another car that created a stir was the Morris Mini – or Austin 7, the British having great brand loyalty – which was introduced in 1959. It was designed by Alec Issigonis and was a truly revolutionary car, with a transverse front-wheel drive engine. It was a reminder that 1950s Britain was still a scientific and industrial power of the first rank. Working with data discovered by British research chemist Rosalind Franklin, Francis Crick and his American colleague James Watson identified the genetic material DNA and its double helix structure, one of the most significant advances of the century. The 'atomic knights', Penney, Hinton and Cockroft, who had brought the country the A-bomb, built the world's first large-scale commercial atomic power station at Calder Hall. Ferranti produced the first commercial computer. ICI led the world in artificial fibres. Christopher Cockerell invented the hovercraft in 1958.

Culturally, it was a creative and varied era, when the gentler side of an older Britain co-existed with the new. Percy Thrower had *Gardening Club* on Friday nights on BBC, an antidote to the teenagers on the pop programmes. The Beverley Sisters and musicals like *Salad Days* and *The Boy Friend* catered for those happy to remain 'squares'. Half a million people might be buying the latest hit records, but 2 million were still going fishing, on rivers, canals and lakes. Others were knitting and keeping budgerigars. As a time of profound but still happy transition, from rationing to plenty, from duty to enjoyment, the Fifties had few equals.

TIMELESS TRIO
The Beverley Sisters were the most popular vocal group in the country and the first British girl group to have a record in the US Top 10. They were real sisters: Joy (in the middle) was the eldest, and twins Teddie and Babs were born on her third birthday. Joy married the footballer Billy Wright, captain of England and the first player to win 100 caps. Their music appealed to family audiences, with songs like *Little Donkey*, *Sisters* and *I Saw Mummy Kissing Santa Claus* among their string of hits. They had their own TV show and topped the bill many times at the London Palladium. In 2002 they entered the Guinness Book of Records as the world's longest surviving unchanged vocal group.

INDEX

PICTURE ACKNOWLEDGEMENTS

Abbreviations: (t) = top; (m) = middle; (b) = bottom; (r) = right; (l) = left

All images in this book are courtesy of Getty Images, including the following which have additional attributions:

6-7 Gerti Deutsch/Getty Images; 12 John Drysdale/Getty Images; 17 John Tarlton/Getty Images; 28(b) Walter Sanders/Time&Life Pictures; 30 Howard Sochurek/Time&Life Pictures; 57 James Burke/Time&Life Pictures; 58(bl) Cornell Capa/Time&Life Pictures; 93(br) Carl Mydans/Time&Life Pictures; 108 W.Eugene Smith/Time&Life Pictures; 116(m) Pix Inc./Time&Life Pictures; 117 Larry Burrows/Time&Life Pictures; 120(br) Eliot Elisofon/ Time&Life Pictures; 124 Alfred Eisenstaedt/Time&Life Pictures; 128 Brian Seed/Time&Life Pictures; 153(tl) 20th Century Fox/Getty Images; 153(tr) Paramount Pictures/Getty Images; 153(b) Columbia Tristar/Getty Images; 156(t) Agence France Presse/Getty Images.

LOOKING BACK AT BRITAIN
ROAD TO RECOVERY – 1950s
was published by The Reader's Digest Association Ltd, London, in association with Getty Images and Endeavour London Ltd.

The Reader's Digest Association Ltd,
11 Westferry Circus
Canary Wharf
London E14 4HE
www.readersdigest.co.uk

First edition copyright © 2007

Endeavour London Ltd
21–31 Woodfield Road
London W9 2BA
info@endeavourlondon.com

Written by
Brian Moynahan

For Endeavour
Publisher: Charles Merullo
Designer: Tea Aganovic
Picture editor: Jennifer Jeffrey

For Reader's Digest
Project editor: Christine Noble
Art editor: Conorde Clarke
Proof-reader: Ron Pankhurst
Indexer: Marie Lorimer
Pre-press account manager: Penelope Grose
Product production manager: Claudette Bramble
Production controller: Katherine Bunn

Reader's Digest General Books
Editorial director: Julian Browne
Art director: Anne-Marie Bulat

Colour origination by Colour Systems Ltd, London
Printed and bound in Europe by Arvato Iberia

We are committed to the quality of our products and the service we provide to our customers.
We value your comments, so please feel free to contact us on 08705 113366, or via our website at:
www.readersdigest.co.uk

If you have any comments or suggestions about the content of our books, you can email us at:
gbeditorial@readersdigest.co.uk

CONCEPT CODE: UK 0154/L/S
BOOK CODE: 638-001 UP0000-1
ISBN: 978 0 276 44249 0
ORACLE CODE: 356900001H.00.24